The Little Spark and
The Great Rays

The Little Spark and The Great Rays

*   *   *

Understanding Your Connection to God with the
Simple Philosophy of A Course In Miracles

ISBN: 0692496270
ISBN 13: 9780692496275

Contents

Foreward by Gary R. Renard

I'm not going to write too long a Foreword for this wonderful book, because I want you to get right to it. Since my first book, *The Disappearance of the Universe*, came out 12 years ago, I've had the privilege of being able to travel and speak, so far in 44 states and 28 countries, about the modern spiritual masterpiece, *A Course In Miracles* (*ACIM*). During that time I've met countless other *Course* teachers.

Much to my surprise, few of these teachers actually understand the *Course*, and thus do not teach it well, which only confuses new students. One of the reasons I wanted to write the Foreword for this book is because its author *does* understand the *Course*, and teaches it in a very gifted way.

I've known Dawn for over ten years, and I've come to realize that her unique, eclectic background, which you will see described in the first half of this book, has helped shape her ability as a spiritual teacher. But the ability to generalize and communicate an advanced and sophisticated thought system like the *Course*, in a comprehensive way that is also simple enough to be approachable to the general public, is a gift that one has to be born with, most likely assisted by experiences that occurred in another time and place, before this dream we call a lifetime.

Wherever that aspect of her ability came from, you'll see in the second part of this book that what Dawn has written is engaging as well as deep. It will give the reader an ability to "get" the *Course* in such a way that they'll be more able to study and apply it. We need all the teachers like that we can get.

I not only enjoyed reading *The Little Spark and The Great Rays*, but I found myself remembering and re-experiencing some of the more mystical excursions Dawn describes from her life. Such experiences are symbolic that the mind is awakening.

I trust that you too will find yourself being lifted to a realm that is available to all, but which can only be achieved by a mind that wants it enough and has the kind of help that is bestowed by both *A Course In Miracles* and this surprising and most helpful book. Enjoy!

Gary R. Renard, best-selling author of *The Disappearance of the Universe* trilogy.

Author's Note

In 2012 I began to write *The Little Spark and The Great Rays*. I had been a student of *A Course In Miracles* for eighteen years when I started to feel a strong urge to write about how it had vastly improved my life. As I sat down to type, it seemed natural that my story, intertwined with lessons from *ACIM*, was destined to be shared with the world.

Part of the impulse to write stemmed from my unique "light experience" which occurred in the spring of 1980.

At the time, I knew something life-changing had happened to me, but I had no frame of reference in which to place it.

I did not realize just how important it was until 1994, after I discovered the true meaning of the *Course*.

My first introduction to this groundbreaking book came in 1989, after I had opened a metaphysical boutique in central Connecticut. My decision to open *Golden Hawk Book & Gift* culminated from years of intense spiritual and intellectual self-discovery, as well as my great desire to share what I had learned with other knowledge seekers.

My intention in opening the store was to help myself and others reach the elusive goals of personal and social transformation, and eventually, Enlightenment.

In the early months of the store's opening, I was often by myself stocking the shelves with the latest New Age titles, such as Louise Hay's *Heal Your Body* and Shakti Gawain's *Creative Visualization*. It was during these quiet times I had the opportunity to peruse another highly regarded book, *A Course In Miracles*.

My first several investigations of *ACIM* left me mystified. I simply couldn't understand it, no matter how hard I tried to concentrate on its many pages. I instinctively knew it was a unique and transcendent book; but I would put it back on the shelf shaking my head in confusion, hoping that its esoteric philosophy would someday become clear to me.

Thankfully, the meaning of the *Course* was revealed shortly after I sold the store to a longtime customer in March of 1994. It was then I discovered the teachings of the inimitable Kenneth Wapnick, PhD. Ken's writings on the *Course* were easily comprehensible, and for the first time I realized the ultimate truth behind my amazing light experience which had been given to me so many years before -- it was nothing less than a Revelation from God!

This little book comprises my reverent and humble attempt to describe in literal terms my personal experience of Revelation. While writing, I have kept in mind there are several passages in the text of *ACIM* advising caution to anyone discussing their own Revelation. The following excerpts make it clear that:

"Revelation is intensely personal and cannot be meaningfully translated. That is why any attempt to describe it in words is impossible."

T1.II.2:1,2

"Revelation is literally unspeakable because it is an experience of unspeakable love."

T1.II.2:7

" ... its content cannot be expressed because it is intensely personal to the mind that received it."

T4.VII.4

These strongly worded admonitions refer to the fact that whenever one writes or speaks about it, mere words will never be enough to communicate the incomparable depth and breadth of this divine Holy Instant. Therefore, you, the reader, will never know what Revelation truly is until you experience it for yourself.

There is another important observation in regard to receiving a Revelation which is found in the Teacher's Manual section of *ACIM*:

> *"It can, perhaps, be won after much devotion and dedication ..."*

M26.3:3

In this passage, we are told that we can "win" a Revelation! It becomes clear the only way to "perhaps" achieve it is by being thoroughly devoted and dedicated. This devotion and dedication is always directed toward God, the Holy Spirit, Jesus, and not least, to all of our brothers and sisters without whom we could not be fully united in Heaven.

Although you will be unable to completely comprehend the experience of Revelation by reading *The Little Spark and The Great Rays*, you can learn the spiritual steps which are recommended prior to attaining one of your own.

By acknowledging your belief in the holy principles presented, and by diligently putting them into practice, you may or may not achieve Revelation in this lifetime. At the very least, you are sure to speed up your spiritual progress and bring yourself that much closer to Enlightenment in this, or a future life. That is my fondest hope.

With the Light of Love,
Dawn of Goldenhawk
Manchester, CT
June, 2015

Acknowledgements

I have been greatly inspired by and motivated to write *The Little Spark and The Great Rays* in large part due to the unwavering dedication and devotion of the following people:

Helen Schucman, PhD, and Bill Thetford, PhD, for their mutual decision to manifest *A Course In Miracles*;

Kenneth Wapnick, PhD, for all of his extraordinary books, seminars, and other materials, which clearly explained the principles of the *Course* to me;

Marilyn Ferguson, whose far-sighted book, *The Aquarian Conspiracy,* allowed me to recognize that I wasn't alone in my unusual beliefs, and that there were millions of like-minded thinkers in the world;

Marianne Williamson, for helping me realize that *ACIM* is a cure for broken people with her healing book, *A Return to Love*;

Gary R. Renard, for revitalizing my study of the *Course* with his charming book, *The Disappearance of the Universe*. I had been *A Course In Miracles* student for ten years by the time I read it, and although *Course* philosophy was never far from my thoughts, my active studies had stalled. *Disappearance* was exactly what I needed to re-ignite the embers of my *ACIM* enthusiasm. For this, Gary, I will always be thankful.

*   *   *

"Reality can dawn only on an unclouded mind. It is always there to be accepted, but its acceptance depends on your willingness to have it. … Knowledge cannot dawn on a mind full of illusions …"

T10.IV.2:1,2,5

About the Author

Dawn of Goldenhawk was born and raised in Hartford County and has been a small business owner, hypnotherapist, lecturer, counselor, and landscape artist in the local area for the past twenty-seven years.

She has been the recipient of many remarkable visions, dreams, and mystical events in her life beginning at six years old, which continue to the present day.

In recent years, Dawn has felt compelled to write her spiritual memoirs, highlighting her experience of Revelation and how powerfully *A Course In Miracles* has affected her life. She is pleased to present it here.

Dedicated With Love
And Gratefulness to
--Jesus Christ—
Our Savior
God's Helper
Our Comforter
The Atonement
The Greatest Teacher
Our Dear Elder Brother
Manifestation of the Holy Spirit
Author of A Course In Miracles

*"Beyond the body, beyond the sun and stars,
past everything you see and yet somehow
familiar, is an arc of golden light that stretches
as you look into a great and shining circle.
And all the circle fills with light before your
eyes."*

T21.I.8:1,2

Introduction

The Little Spark and The Great Rays is based on the philosophy of *A Course In Miracles* and was written with the specific intention of helping you advance to a higher spiritual level by jump-starting your process of achieving Revelation and Enlightenment.

The Little Spark and The Great Rays was written in two parts. In Part One, Chapters 1 – 12 contain a narrative of actual events from the author's life that demonstrate some of the important principles of *ACIM*.

If you are unfamiliar with the *Course*, it is best to first read Chapter 13 in Part Two. It contains a brief, but concise, explanation of its central tenets which are arranged into fifteen simple points and accompanied by quotes from the text.

For a more complete understanding, you can refer to any of the books by Kenneth Wapnick, PhD. You may find *A Talk Given on A Course In Miracles: An Introduction* to be particularly useful. Gary Renard's books and are also of great benefit. In fact most, if not all, of the *ACIM* books on the market today are helpful.

It is important to remember when reading *The Little Spark and The Great Rays* that its wording represents that of *A Course In Miracles*. In *ACIM,* male pronouns such as He and Him, and he and him, are used to describe God, Christ, Holy Spirit, you, me, and the rest of humankind.

As you will learn upon further reading, in Heaven there exists only one infinite Mind created of Light, and in reality, no physical matter, the male and female gender, or forms of any kind, exist at all. Therefore, if the sole use of the male pronoun in the quotes starts to bother you, it is best to keep in mind that gender issues are only important here on earth and not in Heaven, where all is One, and all is the same.

The Little Spark and The Great Rays is intended for several kinds of readers:

- Students of *A Course In Miracles* who seek to understand it at a deeper level, revitalize their studies, or more quickly move along their spiritual path.
- Spiritually minded people who have never studied the *Course* but have heard of it and want to start learning about it.
- Spiritually minded people who have never heard of *ACIM* but may be questioning their

own religion's teachings and would like a better understanding of God and their connection to Him.

Throughout the text of *A Course In Miracles*, circles are used as symbols to describe various concepts such as "the circle of Atonement" and "the holy circle." These circles are to be understood as metaphors and not as physical structures.

The symbol of a circle is also found in *The Little Spark and The Great Rays*, as well as that of the hologram. These symbols are used to represent God, Heaven, and Christ and it was done to help you envision your connection to them. Again, the circle is being used as a learning aid, as a strictly metaphorical representation, and not a literal one.

The author's slightly altered use of capitalization in this book is the only way in which she has differed from the basic presentation of *ACIM*. This was done to put additional emphasis on the sacred ideas presented herein.

*   *   *

"How beautiful indeed are the Thoughts of God who live in his Light! Your worth is beyond perception because it is beyond doubt. Do not perceive yourself in different lights. Know yourself in the One Light where the miracle that is you is perfectly clear."

T3.V.10:6-9

Part One
Revelation and Enlightenment

1

The Revelation of the Little Spark and the Great Rays

"Sometimes a teacher of God may have a brief experience of direct union with God."

M26.3:1

"Revelation unites you directly with God."

T1.II.1:5

"Revelation induces complete but temporary suspension of doubt and fear. It reflects the original form of communication between God and His creations..."

T1.II.1:1,2

"In the Holy Instant, where the Great Rays replace the body in awareness, the recognition of relationships without limits is given you."

T15.IX.3:1

"For in seeing them the body would disappear because its value would be lost."

T16, VI.4:6

When I was twenty-two years old, I had a powerful spiritual experience. It was a beautiful evening in May, and I was resting on my bed after work. My mind was unfocused and drifting lazily when it happened, but I was wide awake and not feeling sleepy or dreaming. I was also not under the influence of any substance.

My apartment in Glastonbury, Connecticut, had cathedral ceilings, and as my gaze floated high into the corner of the room, immense and transparent Rays of white light began to materialize. It seemed as if they were streaming directly from my forehead up to the ceiling.

In that split second, I no longer felt my body. There were no bodily sensations at all. I experienced myself as pure mind, an aware, intelligent mind without a physical body. Then, with some kind of spiritual vision, I "saw" my body become a dark shadow which instantly folded up onto itself. Its shadow became increasingly smaller, and then dropping down as if into a hole, it disappeared entirely.

At that moment I was cognizant of being a singular mind enveloped within a limitless expanse of intensely sparkling golden light. I realized my mind was contained within a larger Mind, a vast and unlimited Mind, which glittered into infinity all around me.

I knew at once that this larger Mind was the Mind of God, and His Mind was the place where Heaven was.

I also knew God had created my mind to live eternally within His Heavenly Mind with Him.

Simultaneously, I felt an incredible sense of all-encompassing Love. The Love emanated the most complete feeling of peace and happiness I had ever experienced. It was utterly exquisite. God's awesome and all-embracing Love comprised the very essence of His Thoughts and wove the glorious, golden fabric of Heaven.

In that same instant, l became aware that there were a limitless number of other minds around me. We were literally brilliant sparkles of light gleaming with the same profound radiance and dwelling as One within the Mind of God. And, although an individual Spark of light illuminated each of our minds, all of our thoughts were exactly the same, and together we functioned as one vast intelligence.

Our thoughts were aligned perfectly with those of our Creator, and there was nothing else to think but His Magnificent Thoughts. And, because our thoughts resonated in perfect unison with God's, it seemed as though there was only one infinite Mind thinking at all.

As my spiritual vision continued to expand, the beautiful light of God which glinted and glowed all around me then became an immense ball, a perfect 360 degree holographic sphere. My mind and all of the other minds God had created along with mine became part of this circular hologram, and we were connected to Him and to the sphere of light by the golden Spark in each of our minds.

I intuitively knew there were no shapes, form, or any kind of physical matter in Heaven, and that the Holy Spirit had placed this analogy of a sphere in my mind to help me understand that our one Mind had always been connected to the eternal light of God and always would be.

His extraordinary Light and Love, and perfect synchronization with all other minds was only part of what I was experiencing in that moment. I was also aware that my mind contained the divine Truth and Knowledge of Heaven, and my knowledge was God's Knowledge. I had no questions; questions were impossible, and didn't exist within His Mind.

The totality of my knowing had no bounds, and I perfectly understood God, myself, and all who lived with us in our radiant Oneness. We were united in an unbreakable bond of everlasting union, and I knew that being in Heaven with God as His Creation was the true meaning of life, and our life together here was truly the meaning of Home.

* * *

Upon my return to normal consciousness, I was astonished. What I felt to be a rare and wondrous event had happened, and I would never look at God, myself, or the world in the same way again. My thoughts were forever stamped with the awesome Revelation of Divine Truth, and from then on I was a changed person.

I had believed in God since childhood, but it was a belief of faith, rather than direct experience. Now I was convinced of God's Reality and felt blessed to have witnessed His, and our, ultimate state of Being.

The major lessons I learned while on my heavenly odyssey was that God is indeed real and is the Creator of my mind and all other minds; there is no physical matter or forms of any kind in Heaven; and we are directly connected to God and to each other by the Light of His Love.

*   *   *

In the weeks after my glimpse of Divinity, I knew it was a stunning gift; but at the same time it began to produce more questions in my mind than it answered. My primary concerns were: why is it we have two homes, one in a dark physical world and another in a world of light? And, why is our matter world connected solely by atoms and sub-atomic particles, rather than by the joyous love and spiritual illumination of our Creator, which is the way heaven is unified?

I had experienced an unparalleled sojourn into Light, where my higher Mind completely understood God and all of His Thoughts, but once I was back to thinking with my earthly mind, the answers to these sobering questions perpetually eluded me.

*   *   *

2

Skidding Back to Earth

"All my brothers are special. If they believe they are deprived of anything, their perception becomes distorted. When this occurs the whole family of God, or the Sonship, is impaired in its relationships."

T.1.V.3:6-8

"... the Holy Spirit uses special relationships,
which you have chosen to support the ego,
as learning experiences that point to truth.
Under His teaching, every relationship
becomes a lesson in love."

T15.V.4:5,6

At the time of my "light experience," as I was calling it then, I was a young woman who was lucky to have been bestowed a rare and sublime blessing, yet whose personal life seemed in worse condition afterward than before it occurred.

I was grateful for the marvelous new perspective, but being a witness to such a beatific event did not ensure my life would automatically become blissful. In fact, many situations became even more difficult on a personal as well as inner level.

The rest of my twenties consisted of a series of roller coaster rides that at times careened out of control and usually ended with a painful bump. I was following the two steps forward and one step back formula in every area as I floundered through young adulthood trying to make sense of life and my place in the world.

I was confronted with health, career, and relationship issues which would take a long time to resolve and push me to the limits of my endurance.

My spiritual beliefs alone kept me moving in a relatively positive direction, although at the time it alarmed me that I still had confusing gaps in my understanding. Consequently, my unanswered questions would continue to fuel the obsessional quest for truth which I had begun as a child.

Looking back later, I realized that my earlier stages of life, including childhood, had been mini "dark nights of the soul," and they were in preparation for the full-fledged dark night which would descend upon me in time.

* * *

While growing up my life was not exactly a picnic, and I felt particularly wretched from ages nine to fifteen.

My parents were from Europe, and they were formal, frugal, and strict with me and my siblings. My father was born in Poland, and my mother was from Ireland. They met while working in a hotel in London after World War II and had emigrated to Connecticut in the mid-1950s.

They were basically good people who encountered many hardships during the war, and it reflected in our upbringing. They provided a clean, well run home but had short tempers and tolerated no nonsense. As often as my parents made us happy, they would make us miserable.

My sister, Ann, was older by ten years, and I worshipped her. When she was in high school, I would iron her clothes and her hair every morning (it was the 1960s), and I would try to spend every moment I could with her. I begged her to allow me into her room, and she would acquiesce, but always after I performed some task. I would massage her back, bring her tea and toast, and stand motionless for an hour on a stool as her artist's model so she could practice drawing.

Ann played with me and protected me, and when I was nine my world was torn apart when she got married and moved to Colorado. After she left, I felt vulnerable, scared, and alone. My parents had each other, as did my two younger brothers, Brian and Paul. I felt like a misfit in my own family and the next several years were dreadful.

My mother had been raised in a staunchly patriarchal Irish village and soon made it known she preferred my brothers. They later confided that she harshly punished me for the same crimes they easily had gotten away with.

She was fiery, sharp-tonged, and narcissistic, and woe to anyone who crossed her. I had to work hard to stay in her good graces, but it was nearly impossible, as I habitually rebelled against the endless chores she demanded I perform. My mom lost her temper with me on a daily basis, and for a few years we were in continual conflict.

My father, having a much less commanding persona, got angry with me a bit less. Little things bothered him, and he would yell at me and my brothers for misdemeanors such as leaving lights on, kitchen cabinets open, or water running too long. He did not enjoy spanking us, however, and every time my mother ordered him to give us the strap, he would hit the bed more than our behinds.

My dad dutifully went to work every day, did not drink or smoke, and gave us a dollar for every "A" on our report cards. Other than that, he stayed behind his newspaper and rarely bothered with us.

He also paid as little attention as he could to my mother; but he did not like to fight with her and went along with whatever she wanted. This tactic proved unfavorable for me, because he would never soften her punishments or veto her bitter decisions regarding my well-being.

The most regrettable consequence of the battles with my mother came when I turned thirteen. She refused to buy clothes for me until I could show some respect. Failing that, I asked my brothers for some of theirs and thereafter endured the humiliation of wearing boy's clothing.

As practically anyone in my position would have, I felt loads of anger and indignation toward my mother for her mistreatment of me. But, even as a young teen I knew that acting on the unpleasant emotions was hurting me, and it certainly was not helping our relationship.

Unsure how to forgive her, I buried the animosity far behind a door labelled "don't go there," and pasting a fake smile on my face, tried to forget my grievances and behave like the daughter my mom wanted me to be.

*   *   *

3

Baby, It's All a Dream

"The Holy Spirit, ever practical in His wisdom, accepts your dreams and uses them as a means for waking."

T18.II.6:1

*"His Light is always the call to awaken,
whatever you have been dreaming."*

T6.V.4:6

As challenging as it was in those early days to handle my mother's ill humor and my own defiant nature, I was able to develop a rich inner life. I often had surprising visions and curious dreams of myself as a different person from other countries and in earlier periods of history. At times I found this confusing and had a hard time grasping why I was being shown scenes of myself living another life.

My first unusual dream came at age six. I awoke frightened and crying after dreaming I was a grown man dying on a prison floor. I could see the filthy cell I was locked in, the vertical bars on the door and the light behind it where the guards were. Strange figures were carved into the wall next to me, stacked one on top of the other.

Later when I was a fairly precocious nine year old, I started to become more interested in religious concepts, including the possibility of past lives. One morning I was leafing through a book on world religions I had found in my parents' cabinet. In the chapter on eastern beliefs, I recognized the carvings from my dream three years earlier. They were called Buddhas.

It hit me that the dream could have been replaying a scene from one of my prior lives -- I must have been a Buddhist and was imprisoned for some reason! This thought immediately triggered a waking vision of myself as a young monk wrapped in orange robes sitting cross legged on the ground. I was surrounded by many other monks, and we were seated in rows facing the front of our temple in the Himalayas waiting for a ceremony to start.

After the proceedings, we filed into a small room inside of our quarters. It had white walls and rows of white boxed compartments, situated on top of benches. Each of us climbed into our own little box, folded our legs underneath us, held our hands in our laps, and closed our eyes.

We were not supposed to fall asleep but many of us did, regularly awakening to the sharp sting of the tiny whip our instructor held.

The book had said Buddhists practiced meditation, a method of quieting the mind, and it was important to their religion. In my vision, our practice of meditation looked and felt so uncomfortable it was difficult for me to believe I would have chosen a lifetime of such discomfort and self-denial.

Though at the time I was sad and forlorn without my sister, I knew the life of that monk must have been even bleaker than mine. He had been removed from his home and the people he loved and was made to perform an awkward and boring practice day after day. As unhappy as I was, after this vision I realized things could be worse.

The next year at age ten, I continued to think about things it didn't seem the adults around me were pondering. Upon awakening in the mornings, I would often ask myself those famous questions,

"Who am I, and why am I here?"

Even at ten years old, I knew there was more to life than everyone was telling me. I just couldn't figure out what it was. I had been having peculiar visions and dreams for several years but was not advanced enough to interpret them. Past lives seemed to be part of the picture, but I was not exactly sure how they fit in. Every year from then on, I would get various hints as to the truth of life, but it would be decades before I could tie all of them together.

In my tenth year I had another past life experience that looking back on as an adult, perhaps helped to explain why Revelation came to me in this lifetime. One afternoon while I was playing in my bedroom, I had another brief, but powerful, past life vision. I saw myself as an older man wearing a green velvet cape and matching green stockings holding a palette and paintbrush. I was standing in front of a huge mural on which I had been working. Though the vision lasted only a short while, it was very clear, and I was perplexed by it.

It wasn't until I was twenty-nine when I discovered the man's identity. I happened to have a psychic reading by a woman who channeled the ascended master, Djwhal Kuhl. During the reading, I was shocked to learn that I had been Giotto di Bondone, one of the first painters of the Renaissance. I had never heard of him before and went straight to the library after the reading to discover what I could about the artist.

Giotto was a devout Catholic from Vespignano, Italy, who had painted many altarpieces and murals of the life of Jesus Christ. His most famous works are the frescoes which hang in the Arena Chapel in Padua and in the Uffizi Gallery in Florence. Giotto is still renowned in the art world for the first use of correct perspective in painting.

The reading explained my love of art and painting and my devotion to Jesus in this current lifetime.

I had always felt close to Jesus since a little girl. At four, I was brought to church every Sunday by my Irish Catholic mother, and by six I was faithfully attending catechism on Saturday mornings. I made my First Communion at seven and was confirmed a full Catholic before my eleventh birthday. Each week in church, I would look up at Jesus on his cross, thankful he got rid of my sins but not happy he had to suffer so much in the process.

Soon after my Catholic Confirmation, my mother unexpectedly converted to the B'ahai Faith. A gentle religion, it originated in Persia (Iran) in the mid-1800s, and some of its tenets are the belief in one omniscient God who created all things in the universe, all humans are equal to each other, and that human consciousness is slowly evolving toward unity, peace, and justice on a worldwide level.

There are currently over five million B'ahais, and they practice their religion in small, weekly study groups known as "firesides." These meetings are held in the private homes of practitioners, and when one of my mother's acquaintances invited her to a local fireside, it was there that she found her new faith.

Soon after her conversion, early one Sunday morning my mom came into my room while I was getting dressed and made a dramatic announcement, her thick brogue swirling around my ears. I could go back to bed; we would not be attending church anymore.

What? I was baffled because my mother had always been so rigid about our weekly pilgrimage to Saint Margaret Mary's. I was not sure I liked the idea, but on the other hand, the thought of sleeping later on Sundays was secretly appealing.

I knew from then on I would have to keep Jesus in my heart because I wouldn't be seeing him as much in person.

I hoped he would understand.

*   *   *

I continued to have past life dreams and sudden waking visions throughout the rest of my tenth year.

I saw myself as a Native American of Lakota Sioux heritage living on the Plains, and another time as a middle class wife and mother of ten from a large American city in what looked to be the 1930s.

I had an especially startling dream wherein I was an affluent country gentleman living in England in the 1700s.

I was tall, thin, and impeccably dressed in a pale blue satin jacket, waistcoat, and breeches. A matching tricorn hat sat atop my grey powdered wig.

I was married and had an ill wife. We lived on a remote, but idyllic, large estate with well-kept lawns and vibrant gardens.

The part of my mind that was conscious during the dream knew my wife was my sister from this life, and I realized she was not physically sick at all. She was depressed. Her long, dark curls descended from an elaborate bun, and she wore an exquisite white organdy gown with accordion pleats and tiny embroidered bluebells.

She was reclined on a porch swing on our veranda crying miserably because I was leaving on a long trip and would not be able to take her with me. In the last scene of the dream, my wife was begging me not to go, and I was standing next to the swing trying to console her, without success.

When I awakened, I wondered if it had anything to do with my sister leaving home the year before. Because of this dream, I began to suspect that what happens in one lifetime may have something to do with what happens in another.

4

Walking the Tightrope of Karma

"In the ultimate sense, reincarnation is impossible. There is no past or future, and the idea of birth into a body has no meaning either once or many times."

M24.1:1,2

"Reincarnation cannot, then, be true in any real sense. Our only question should be, "Is the concept helpful?" And that depends, of course, on what it is used for. If it is used to strengthen the recognition of the eternal nature of life, it is helpful indeed ..."

M24.1:3-6

Near the end of my tenth year, I had a significant dream which would frighten me for a long time afterward and that I would continue to think about years later. The dream began innocently enough, in a scene where I was my normal ten year old self walking along the road in front of our house, as I was often wont to do as a kid.

Before long, I realized someone was in back of me, and I turned around to see who it was. A wealthy looking, elegantly dressed man was seated in an orange lounge chair gliding jauntily along behind me. He wore a black tuxedo jacket and pants with a crisp white shirt and a black bowtie.

The chair was one of those adjustable loungers with woven plastic strips popular in the 1960s. The man seemed happy and relaxed and was somehow propelling it along, trailing my steps.

I was horrified to see the man had no face. There was instead a totally blank, stark white mannequin's head where his facial features should have been.[1] I let out a shriek and started to walk faster. But the faster I walked, the faster he drove the lounge chair behind me. I couldn't lose him no matter how fast or far I went.

At that point I woke up sweating and quaking in fear. I had to sleep in my parents' room for the rest of the night. I couldn't stop worrying that the man would come back. I became afraid of the dark and suffered terrible insomnia, awake and vigilant, fearful of his return. It had been a shocking dream that haunted my childhood, shaking my feelings of basic safety.

Over time I gradually got over the fear; but I never forgot him, and talked about the "man in the orange lounge chair" with anyone who would listen. It wasn't until decades later I was finally able to discern the meaning of the dream. One day I kept getting an overwhelming feeling that I was the man in the orange lounge chair – he was *me* from a past life! I then started to get flashes of disturbing details from that life.

I had been an affluent man of aristocratic birth who lived in Paris in the late 1800s. I was an accomplished artist who was fawned over by the people in my social circle and held in awe by those of lower status. I had a highborn pedigree and flawless manners, but I was a consummate narcissist and lived life solely for my own pleasure. I treated others with a cavalier disregard for

---

[1] I had this dream in 1968, forty-one years before a similar looking fictional character known as Slenderman first appeared as an internet meme in 2009.

their happiness and peace of mind. I had many love affairs and wherever I went left behind a wake of brokenhearted lovers and their outraged family members.

I should have been regarded by my peers as the rogue I was, but due to my noble breeding and considerable talent, those around me pretended not to notice my callous behavior. At the time, the upper classes got away with the most heinous of social inequities, and I was no exception.

The last vision I had of myself as that man was in the afterlife of his lifetime. I saw myself sitting in a dark room in front of a large projection screen. To my right was a long table where several wise and holy teachers were assembled, watching the movie of my life with me. Seated in the middle was Jesus Christ.

The life I had just left was playing itself out in the most minute detail before us. And, even though I saw myself so often being cruel and indifferent to the feelings of others, I didn't seem to care. I watched while slouched in my chair in a position of utmost nonchalance, my right ankle casually resting on my left knee. My superior, egotistical attitude from that lifetime seemed fully intact during the life review.

While contemplating the scene, my present day conscious mind was astounded I could be so haughty and disdainful even while in front of Jesus and the other celestial beings.

After the vision was over, and I was back to my normal waking consciousness, I felt ashamed I had cast aside kindness and compassion in favor of domination and control. I was dismayed that I had chosen to be so heartless in one of my most recent past lives, and it felt even worse to know I had stubbornly clung to those disagreeable character traits in the afterlife.

On the other hand, it felt good to finally know why the faceless man had relentlessly pursued me, both in the dream and in my thoughts for years afterward. His frightening legacy was there to remind me that I had chosen my current lifetime to balance negative karma with forgiveness and good deeds, making right the wrongs I had committed so long ago. With that peek into my self-indulgent past, it was now easy to understand why I had encountered a marked lack of empathy by certain family members, friends, and significant others during my present life.

Until that eye-opening glimpse, I was of the belief that I had incarnated as a good person for at least the last few centuries. The vision disproved my romantic notion of having had many virtuous prior lifetimes. I speculated that I must have spent some time relearning important spiritual doctrines and recommitting to loftier ideals in between that life of egocentric hedonism and the incarnation to follow.

After discovering the meaning of the dream, I was reminded by my *ACIM* studies that our beliefs in time, this life, past lives, and the afterlife, are all different forms of the false ideas of the collective ego.

Past lives are no more real than our present lifetime is, but because we believe that we are living here now, and that we have also lived other lives, it is necessary to forgive our mistaken conviction in the passage of time.

We need only remember the real and true state of our being resides in the eternity of heaven, and not in an unpredictable universe where death and time rule with a clock's iron hand.

*   *   *

5

My Guide and the Land of Goldenhawk

*"Across the bridge it is so different! For a time
the body is still seen, but not exclusively, as it
is seen here. The little Spark that holds the
Great Rays within it is also visible, and this
Spark cannot be limited long to littleness."*

T16.VI.6:1-3

*"There are those who have reached God
directly, retaining no trace of worldly limits
and remembering their own Identity perfectly.
These might be called the Teachers of teachers
because, although they are no longer visible,
their image can yet be called upon. And they
will appear when and where it is helpful for
them to do so."*

M26.2:1-3

Fortunately, none of my subsequent youthful dreams were as nerve-rattling as that of the lounge chair man. Enough fear had been installed into my brain by that time, and I could not bear more. The next several years happily brought no nightmares, and instead, my dream scenarios were of a benign or pleasing nature.

Shortly after I turned fourteen, the most influential dream of my life occurred. It seemed profoundly real. In it, I was introduced to my heavenly guide, and he took me on an amazing journey to a sacred place; a nirvana beyond time, karma, and reincarnation.

My guide was an entity of pure golden light. Shining beams radiated from his entire being, and I felt a male energy from him rather than female. He had on a long flowing robe and the only parts of his body that weren't covered were his head, hands, and feet. He was hovering slightly above the ground in front of me, tall and luminous. I was enchanted by his countenance of gleaming gold. Looking up at him, I wished that I, too, could shine with such incredible brilliance.

My guide placed the thought in my mind that he was going to take me on an important trip and then lifted me out of bed and put me under his arm. We flew out of my bedroom in the heart of Connecticut and headed westward over the U.S.

I looked down at the rolling pastures, hills, fields, rivers, and the lights of the towns and cities going rapidly by below. We were flying effortlessly in the dark, and the night was lit by the stars. I felt no fear.

About three-quarters across the country, over what I estimated to be Idaho, we came to a place where the countryside shimmered with the same warm radiance as my guide's. The scene was breathtakingly beautiful.

Stately mountains circled the horizon, and gently swaying wheat was planted all the way to the foreground. The sky beyond glowed softly with ethereal sunlight.

My guide stopped over the large wheat field, and I saw several luminescent beings below us tenderly caring for the plants. Like my enchanting guide, they appeared ageless and were flawlessly perfect in their golden resplendence.

They were also joyously happy. The happiness they exuded was palpable, and their thoughts were of the purest vibrations of truth. They had no secrets or parts of their minds that were closed off from one another.

Their love for God, each other, and all of God's creations was total, unconditional.

After I had taken in the majestic landscape with a gasp, my guide relayed his thoughts to me, saying,

"This is the land of Goldenhawk, and it is your destiny. It is a place of timeless perfection and is the bridge to Heaven. Because there is no death or decay here, every leaf, blade of grass, and sheaf of wheat is unblemished.

Everyone and everything here lives eternally and shines with God's holy light. The divine beings who reside here are beyond time but know they are not yet in heaven. As there is no past or future in this land, only an eternal now, there is no sense of waiting.

He continued,

"Many of the inhabitants of Goldenhawk have ascended here from the dark world where you believe you now live.

Others have come from different worlds. But they were all able to stop the seemingly inexorable wheel of karma after learning to forgive their own and others' mistakes, and to love wholly equally. They chose to ignore the ego and its temptations and listen only to the Holy Spirit. This was usually after many lifetimes of practice. When there were no more lessons to learn, they became enlightened and ended the illusory cycle of their physical lives.

After a brief pause, my guide again gently spoke to me with his mind,

"As each ascends here, there is a joyous celebration, and when the last separated mind in the material universe has finally arrived, we all will be carried back to heaven by God. There is a grand plan at work to help make this happen, and the one you know as Jesus Christ is in charge of it.

My guide went on,

"Enlightenment is a goal you, too, are going to reach, but your work is not yet over. You have done well in preparing for it during a number of prior lifetimes you believe that you have lived, but how well you do in your present life will determine how quickly you return to Goldenhawk."

My teenage mind was reeling both from what my guide had been communicating and from the glowing panorama stretching in front of me. He told me that I was destined to come back and live in this splendid place!

At that point the dream ended, and I found myself back in my bed, startled but very excited. I soon fell into a deep and refreshing sleep. When I awakened the next morning, I remembered the dream instantly.

The radiant beauty of Goldenhawk and its inhabitants was imprinted on my mind, and I knew it must have been more than just a dream. I believed it was an actual visit from my spiritual guide and thus was especially important to my life.

I got up and dressed within minutes so I could run to school early and check the atlas and world book in the library for a place called Goldenhawk. I arrived in record time and poured over the maps of Idaho trying to find it.

When I couldn't find it there, I looked all over the world but was just as unsuccessful. I wondered where this mystical locale might be. Due to youthful naivety, it never occurred to me that Goldenhawk was not part of the physical world and could not be found on any map.

In the weeks following my visit, I was barely able to pay attention to parents or teachers. I constantly daydreamed of my astounding adventure and desperately wanted to repeat it.

I wondered why my guide had chosen me, a shy and awkward teen, to be taken to a fantastic Shangri La that saints and wise men spend their lives searching for. I knew that I was unusually sensitive to unexplained phenomena, but this dream seemed to be from another realm entirely.

I was grateful for the incomparable experience, but at the same time felt I really couldn't do much with it. Once again, I talked to anyone who would listen but was powerless to impress those around me. My family amusingly dismissed the enormity of my vision as an imaginative fantasy. Goldenhawk was not understood for the goldmine it was, and it soon became a castle in the air, tantalizingly out of my reach.

Afterward, the pressures of adolescence and a rocky relationship with my demanding mother consumed me.

I no longer had time for spiritual matters, and the influence of my lovely guide and his uplifting message gradually faded.

I was not gifted with a miracle of the same magnitude until the day of my Revelation eight years later. My guide took a little longer to return; I would not see him again for twenty years.

*   *   *

6

Laying the Groundwork for Revelation

"Truth has rushed to meet you since you called upon it."

T18.III.3:1

"...you will advance, because your goal is the advance from fear to Truth. The goal you accepted is the goal of knowledge, for which you signified your willingness."

T18.III.2:2,3

"Consciousness is the receptive mechanism, receiving messages from above or below, from the Holy Spirit or the ego. Consciousness has levels, and awareness can shift quite dramatically ... At its highest, it becomes aware of the real world and can be trained to do so increasingly."

C1.7:3-5

Life became easier in my later teen years. I had grown graceful and confident, found a comfortable place among my peers, and even entered into a delicate truce with my mother.

I was still asking the big questions but this time turned to psychology rather than spirituality to look for answers. I joined my school's psychology club and, due to my inquisitive temperament, found the study of psychological concepts thoroughly compelling.

We were assigned various books to read, and I studied Freud's theory of the id, ego, and superego, and Jung's essays on dreams. These were topics of ceaseless fascination and answered some of the questions I had been puzzling over in regard to human nature.

After reading *Gestalt Therapy* by Fritz Perls, I realized there were parts of my world I had never noticed before, and seeing them depended on where I put my attention.

I learned that I could glean new information from my environment either by concentrating on the figures in the foreground of a scene, or by looking farther into the distance, to the background. Perceiving the figure and the ground individually gave me a unique perspective on both; one I could not obtain by viewing them together, which is the usual way our minds and eyes work.

After that, my school club began exploring the subject of hypnotism, and it seemed particularly captivating. I watched my teachers take turns hypnotizing each other, and in one instance a female teacher was brought back to five years old. It was uncanny how she spoke with the innocence and intonation of a little girl.

My teachers asked if any of us students wanted to be hypnotized, and I promptly volunteered. Since it was against the law to put a student into a state of full hypnosis, they could take me only part of the way.

I felt the initial stages of hypnotic induction to be so relaxing, one of my teachers suggested I try meditation. She said it was a form of self-hypnosis I could practice at home. I told her I had heard of it.

I borrowed a book on meditation from the library and read that a light meditative state evoked pleasant feelings similar to hypnosis. Deeper levels could produce a sense of euphoria, and it was linked to spirituality as a way to commune with the divine.

I remembered from my earlier foray into Buddhism that the daily practice of meditation and contemplation was how the Buddha had reached Enlightenment.

My youthful vision of the fledgling monk meditating in his little box also returned to my mind, and I thought it could be the reason I was so drawn to hypnosis. Though meditation seemed difficult and uncomfortable for him, he may have eventually mastered it.

Hypnosis and meditation are both techniques that enable us to reach the alpha brainwave state. In alpha, our consciousness is relaxed and open to information from our right mind, the dwelling place of the Holy Spirit. The reflection of God's Joy and Knowledge reaches us easily when our brains are pulsing with calming alpha waves. While in alpha, pleasurable feelings are enhanced and ideas arise that are on a heightened cognitive level.

In addition to alpha, science has determined there are four other brainwave types. They are beta, theta, delta, and the most recently discovered, gamma.

Beta, our brainwave state of everyday consciousness, is not a reliable conduit for higher thoughts and feelings as it is readily subject to influence from wrong minded thoughts of the ego. It is difficult, therefore, for highly refined impulses to emerge when we are in the beta state.

While in beta, the ego is in control and is never re-laxed. Its mode is one of hypervigilance, constantly on the defensive for all perceived attacks. The ego is the part of our personality which believes in a "dog eat dog world." We are aligned with the ego anytime we are fearful, angry, sad, anxious, annoyed, indifferent, or focused on any number of other pessimistic thoughts and emotions.

The Holy Spirit's right-minded insight and happiness becomes available when we deliberately choose to set aside negative perceptions. Our choice to repeatedly do this takes awareness and practice and is one of the best ways we can devote and dedicate ourselves to listening to Him.

Gamma waves also appear to produce an openness to the Holy Spirit's higher wisdom, but the slower cycling theta and delta waves are associated with the unconscious mind and sleep. They are realms of the ego, though in these states it does not have as tight a hold on our resting mind, and at times the Holy Spirit can speak to us through uplifting dreams.

*   *   *

7

Where, Oh Where, is My Utopia?

"This Course does not attempt to take from you the little that you have. It does not try to substitute utopian ideas for satisfactions which the world contains.

WpI.133.2:3,4

*"God's word has promised that peace is
possible here, and what He promises can
hardly be impossible. But it is true that the
world must be looked at differently ..."*

M11.1:7,8

My teenage explorations into psychology and hypnosis
helped to shape my expanding worldview, and it was
undeniable that I had been growing intellectually and
spiritually at a steady rate since childhood.

By the time I was twenty, I had evolved into an
open minded, idealistic, and deep thinker. I believed peace on earth was possible and that humankind could live in harmony if only we would embrace
the concepts of tolerance and equality. Daydreams
of what it would be like to live in a peaceful world
occupied my mind, and I was soon consumed by the
idea of a utopian civilization where we all tranquilly
coexisted.

I endeavored to read everything I could about utopian societies which had been founded over the centuries, and the Essenes from ancient Israel intrigued me.
They were priests and healers who believed in spiritual
practice and the brotherhood of man, and upon enter-
ing the order, took a vow of poverty.

Unfortunately, the ancient world was not ready to
accept the Essene way of life. They were vanquished

to the pages of history when their largest enclave was destroyed by the Romans in 68 AD.

By studying more recent examples of intentional communities, I discovered humankind was still a long way from the utopian ideal. I read about nineteenth century collaborative ventures established in the U.S., such as Oneida in New York and the various Shaker villages scattered around the mid-west and New England. Though they were tolerant and progressive, these settlements endured an ever dwindling membership, indicating their general lack of appeal. They were guaranteed to be failed experiments.

I also looked into twentieth century utopias, and in the early 1980s even visited two of them. Both places had based their version of utopia on popular books and did their best to embody the central principles of egalitarianism, which are equality and shared resources. In fact, both did an admirable job of representing these objectives.

The first commune I visited was the now defunct Kerista Village, formerly located in the Haight-Ashbury district of San Francisco. The founders based their vision of communal life on Robert Heinlein's *Stranger in a Strange Land*, published in 1961.

My initial impression of the members was as a ragtag bunch of hippies. My opinion was colored by their macramé vests, shredded bellbottoms, and untidy crash pad, but contrary to what I expected, they proved to be intellectual and highly articulate.

The second co-op I called on was Twin Oaks in western Virginia, established in 1967. It was fashioned after the mythical commonwealth in *Walden Two*, published in 1948 by the famous American behaviorist, B.F. Skinner. Somewhat surprisingly, Twin Oaks has managed to duplicate *Walden Two's* cooperative lifestyle quite well, and this thriving collective is still in full operation today.

I briefly toyed with the idea of moving to one of these communities, but an obstacle for me was the fact that a spirit-centered lifestyle was not a goal of either location. They were more rooted in the practical side of life; where to live, how to support themselves, obtain food, divide chores, take care of health needs, etc.

The communards were also free to experiment sexually. Keristans practiced polyfidelity (sexual faithfulness to more than one lover), and Twin Oakers seem to practice any kind of sexual combinations they want, including monogamy.

Not that there is anything wrong with people engaging each other in such ways if they are inclined, but I wished to live in a more spiritually conscious setting where metaphysical ideals and a reduction of ego gratification were main goals, not in the background. It was obvious neither environment was right for me.

Thereafter, I was forced to conclude my personal foray into utopianism was unsuccessful. What I was seeking did not seem to exist. I reasoned that our planet's vast diversity of cultures and religions guaranteed we would not be able to live together in such an idealized way on a mass scale.

Also, many people I knew felt utopian concepts smacked too much of Communism and totalitarianism – very unpopular ideas in a Western thought system.

My belief that world peace could be achieved through the global adoption of an egalitarian lifestyle was dashed. Reluctantly, I abandoned my goal of living in an intentional society and returned to a path geared more toward individual growth.

What I didn't know at the time was that my intense longing for all people of the world to live peacefully and cooperatively had been preparing my mind for a Revelation.

Eventually, I would come to realize through my studies of the *Course* that peace *is* possible in this world if everyone on the planet chose to listen to the Holy Spirit instead of his or her ego.

* * *

> " ... *an open mind can hear the Call to waken. It is not shut tight against God's Voice. It has become aware that there are things it does not know* ... "

WPI.169.3:4-6

During my late teens and early twenties, my passionate investigation of dreams, spirituality, past lives, psychology, utopianism, world peace, and the practice of self-hypnosis, meditation, and Gestalt exercises, opened my mind to the possibility of direct communication with a higher source, and it was the pursuit of these courses of study and practice that laid the groundwork for the attainment of my reunion with God.

By age twenty-one, my mind had broadened so much I began to access information of a universal nature, and I wondered if this material was from my higher self or perhaps even my golden guide.

I took to lying quietly on my bed with a pen and paper and would write down anything I felt was coming from the divine part of my mind. The material that came through was often about the light and darkness of our physical world, the higher and lower attributes of mankind, and the interconnectedness of all things.

As much as I enjoyed reflecting on these subjects and knew they were intimately related, I was unable to combine them into a coherent philosophy of life that gave me solid answers. Despite an intense pursuit of truth, I was forced to admit there still existed giant holes in my comprehension which refused to be patched. I stored the information in the back of my mind along with everything else I had learned in the preceding years, and prayed for Enlightenment.

Little did I know that by spring of the next year, my mind would be altered forever, and I would come much closer to cracking open the mysterious egg of life.

My acquisition of a "universal mindset" is what I believe ultimately cleared the way for God to reveal Himself to me. The fervent wish to live in peace with all people, the decision to open my mind to higher learning, and a fierce drive to possess divine knowledge is what at last made it possible.

*   *   *

8

Metaphysics and the New Age

"We only start again an ancient journey long ago begun that but seems new. We have begun again upon a road we travelled before and lost our way a little while. And now we try again."

CEP. 3:2-4

*"Our new beginning has the certainty the
journey lacked till now."*

CEP. 3:5

Several months after my voyage to Heaven, I read
Marilyn Ferguson's landmark book, *The Aquarian
Conspiracy.* It was because of this book I discovered
there were millions of people across the globe who
had spiritual beliefs similar to mine, and that I was not
alone in my thinking.

Ms. Ferguson talked of multitudes of seekers who were
in the midst of a 'paradigm shift' in consciousness. For a
few hundred years, this shift has been pushing people away
from the traditional view of a predictable and measurable
Newtonian universe to that of a holographic and fluid
one based on metaphysical laws instead of mechanics.

Ever since the evolutionary triumph of higher consciousness started to manifest itself in the human psyche,
this new epoch in thought has allowed humans to break
long held barriers to intellectual and spiritual progress
and move forward into the light of knowledge and truth.

We have finally bred into our minds to a vast degree
the ability to see past the veils of fear and denial which
initially propelled us to come to this world of death and decay. Humankind has stepped onto a higher threshold, and

we have been looking at ourselves in a new way ever since: as unlimited, multi-dimensional beings capable of healing our false perceptions of ourselves and the universe.

In Ms. Ferguson's book title, the word *Aquarian* refers to the Age of Aquarius. It is one of twelve 2,167 year astronomical ages that make up a 26,000 year cycle in the Earth's orbit. This cycle is known as a Great Year and is based on the precession of the equinoxes. The Aquarian Age replaced the prior Piscean Age; therefore, it is also known as the New Age.

"New Age" has become the umbrella term for the various metaphysical philosophies which have filtered into humankind's collective unconscious since the start of the paradigm shift. Any ideology is considered to be New Age if it is outside the realm of everyday understanding and acceptance.

By the 1980's, the New Age had gained steam as a vital, living movement fully out in the open, and its doctrines were no longer being kept hidden in the secret reading rooms of past centuries.

Although science has not yet exactly pinpointed when the earth moved into the Aquarian Age, I like to believe it officially began on December, 21, 2012, in alignment with the end of the Mayan calendar.

* * *

In the months and years following my heavenly Revelation and discovery of New Age Thought, I became hesitant to disclose my extraordinary, light-filled vision to anyone who did not appear to believe in anything beyond the physical.

It was comforting to know I had a fascinating secret I suspected most people didn't have, but the several times I spoke of it to my friends or family, I again got incredulous looks or cheeky comments that it must have been my imagination going wild. As in earlier times, I found it impossible to convince anyone of the reality or importance of my deeply felt inner experience.

By my mid-twenties, I gave up trying to convince the skeptics around me that there was much more to life than what they could see or touch. Instead, I decided to make contact with others who believed the same way I did; I just didn't know where to look.

I would meet people here and there who had similar notions, but it wasn't until one day in 1986, while in a neighborhood health food store, I discovered there were thousands of like-minded thinkers right here in Connecticut.

I picked up a networking magazine called *The Door Opener* founded by a New Age proponent named Jon Roe, and it introduced the local metaphysical community to me.

The magazine is still being published, currently by Dory Dzinski, and it lists dozens of individual practitioners, organizations, and retail stores in the region dedicated to the many branches of spirituality, metaphysics, and healing. It serves as a vehicle linking individuals and groups who are committed to pursuing a lifestyle of holistic health and spiritual growth.

At the time, I was excited to learn there were so many higher minded thinkers in my area, and I finally felt part of a welcoming community that not only understood, but embraced, my esoteric beliefs.

From then on I made it my task to visit as many of the New Age stores and groups listed in the Door Opener as possible. I spent countless satisfying hours among bookshelves reading up on obscure thought systems and attending talks on meditation, spirit guides, Native American religions, auric healing, crystal energy, reincarnation, feng shui, medicine animals, out of body and near death experiences, Wicca, shamanism, and numerous other mysterious and arcane subjects.

I found solace in meeting fellow believers and knowing I was in good company in my uncommon thinking. The only thing that surprised me about my New Age friends was not one seemed to have encountered the same kind of light event I had. Certainly, no one thought I was weird or making it up, but I never once met anyone who had experienced it. No matter, like everything else that confounded me about life, I put it on a shelf in my mind and tried not to let it bother me.

*   *   *

Instead, I decided to focus my mind on things my parents had been endlessly pressuring me to do: finish my degree, choose a career, save money, and get married. The first three goals I agreed with wholeheartedly; the last item I wasn't so sure about.

Two years before, my boyfriend of eight years, and recent fiancé, was caught philandering while I was in traction in the hospital. I had been in a car accident which shattered my hip, and my healing process took almost an entire year. He grew restless waiting for me to recover, and then he got careless.

A dear family friend named Marilyn found out about his indiscretions told my parents. My mother sat me down the very first day I could walk again and relayed what Marilyn had confided. She worked in the same office as the woman whom my fiance had been pursuing, and it turned out he was practically stalking the poor lady. The woman had to rebuff his advances repeatedly.

The information had sent my mother into a tailspin, and she forbade me to let him darken our door ever again.

Somehow I found it easy to forgive him, but I was forced to call off the wedding. It didn't make sense to marry a man with whom my parents refused to associate.

After that romantic debacle, I thought maybe it would be best to stay single. Going back to college and finding a rewarding job seemed much easier in comparison to getting married.

During the next few years, I continued to pursue the study of metaphysics but also took steps to gain a mainstream career which would bring me the secure and abundant life I wanted. I had always felt that to be rich in spirit didn't mean I should be poor in person, and I was willing to put in the hard work necessary to attain my share of middle class comfort.

In a wave of overreaching ambition, I enrolled in full time college courses in both art and business, and at the same time worked forty hour weeks as a staff accountant at a nearby insurance company. This demanding schedule was tiring, but I always found time to contemplate my mystical union with God and universal beliefs.

I managed to grow inwardly strong during those grueling years as I scraped together the bits of esoteric wisdom that made sense to me, and I made it through my late twenties without too many dings and dents.

In the same period, a friend introduced me to the man who would become my husband. So much for staying single.

*   *   *

9

Adventures in Retail

*"Those who have developed "psychic" powers
have simply let some of the limitations they
laid upon their minds be lifted."*

M25.6.7

*"Who transcends these limits in any way is
merely becoming more natural. He is doing
nothing special, and there is no magic in his
accomplishments."*

M25.2.7,8

*"The seemingly new abilities that may be
gathered along the way can be very helpful.
Given to the Holy Spirt, and used under His
direction they are valuable teaching aids."*

M25.3.1,2

In 1989, a year after I got married, I grew bored working in a career I wasn't passionate about and decided to open a book store.

I thought it would be thrilling to combine my business skills with my New Age interests, and in just a few months opened Golden Hawk Book & Gift in Southington, CT. The motto I advertised on my business cards was "Working for Personal and Social Transformation."

My New Age store carried books on metaphysics, meditation supplies, crystals and stones, music, incense, and many other spiritually oriented items. They were intended to enhance one's awareness of God, self, and the universe.

One of the main attractions of the store was an eyes open meditation booth, called the Star Chamber. It was a square, four foot high wooden box lined with mirrors and had a hemi-synch sound system attached.

The idea was to sit inside and, while keeping one's eyes open, achieve the alpha brainwave. The music in the booth worked to synchronize the left and right brain hemispheres while the mirrors flooded the optic nerves with thousands of images. The combined effect allowed one to obtain the meditative state much faster than by the usual procedures.

Not one to avoid my share of uncommon experiences, the Star Chamber soon provided me with breathtaking images, and especially unforgettable was the time my face transformed into that of Jesus. He was beautiful, and I stared straight into his fathomless eyes.

Interestingly, there was another person who saw Jesus in the chamber. Of the hundreds of customers who went in, just one reported seeing his face. I thought it was cool I was not alone.

During the five years I owned the store, I honed my public speaking skills by teaching classes on dreams, spirit animals, and reincarnation. I became a Certified Hypnotherapist and performed past life regressions for thirty people at a time. I built a sound proof room in my home and saw private hypnosis clients outside of store hours. Over six hundred of them floated away to alpha state on my couch.

I also offered readings to people who wanted a peek into their past, present, and future. I used a variety of stones and crystals which spoke to me, as well as clients' animal guides to glean insight into their lives. In addition, I used Tarot cards to make sure I gave a particularly well-rounded reading.

I was familiar with the Tarot while growing up, because my mother used to read them for family and friends. She had a natural ability to know what they meant, and as a teen, I was spellbound by what she could see in them.

Later on, I realized that I had inherited her talent to see the coincidences and patterns in the cards which could tell a story about a person.

> " ... we but see the journey from the point at which it ended, mentally reviewing what has gone by."

WPI.158.4:5

As *A Course In Miracles* teaches, all humans have inherent psychic capabilities and can see the future if desired. We can do this not only because psychic ability is a naturally occurring power of our minds, but also because all time and events have already transpired, and are still imprinted in our unconscious memories.

*   *   *

One of the perks that came with owning a New Age store was free advertising in the form of newspapers, radio programs, and television stations wanting to do human interest stories. I agreed to participate in every one of them, because as soon as a piece on the store was printed or aired, it brought in slews of new customers.

In January of 1993, I got a request for an interview from WTNH, a local television station. Ellen Abrams, the news anchor, was preparing a story on the New Age movement and the increasing popularity of psychic readings. During the interview, she asked me to do a Tarot spread for her.

Ellen was beautiful, confident, and skeptical of anything that science couldn't explain. Instantly, I sensed her take on the segment would be geared toward denouncing my 'crackpot' beliefs. As I was used to some people thinking I was an oddball, Ellen's agenda didn't faze me. And, being the practical business person I was, the free publicity was too lucrative to pass up.

Regardless of where I went, there was always a certain percentage of New Age naysayers, and I had learned long before to ignore them. They were not my target customer base and wouldn't be coming into my store after the piece was shown anyway, so I sat down with Ellen to do her reading with little hesitation. She motioned for her equally dubious videographer to train his oversized camera on us.

When we got comfortable around a small table, I gave Ellen an open deck of Rider Waite cards; the same brand my mother used. I also used the same seven card spread in my readings as my mom did: the first three cards are placed on the left in front of the questioner and represent the past, the middle card signifies the present, and the three cards on the right symbolize the future.

I asked Ellen to shuffle the deck as much or as little as she wanted and to randomly pick the seven cards needed for the reading, placing them face down in a straight row in front of her. I then instructed her to turn over each card so it lay face up.

When she finished, what I saw in the cards made me shiver. Of the hundreds of readings I had given through the years, and had watched my mother give, never before had the same combination of cards been chosen. I racked my brain for what they possibly could mean because my rational mind refused to accept the message that seemed to be presenting itself in front of me: physical death.

I tried to stifle my dismay, told Ellen that I thought the cards were not very positive, and suggested we use a brand new deck. Grabbing at straws, I told her that maybe she was allowing her doubts and negative thinking about psychic readings to permeate her cards?

I took a new deck off a nearby rack, asked Ellen to open them and go through same procedure as before.

To my utter shock and disbelief, the exact same cards in the exact same order were staring up at me from the table when she was done. The cards from left to right were: 3 of Swords, 5 of Swords, 8 of Swords, 9 of Swords, 10 of Swords, Death, and the Tower.

The Death card frequently shows up in readings and people are always concerned, but the card by itself never means physical death. It signifies the ending or transformation of some situation in the person's life, not the end of their physical body. But this time, because of the dire combination of the other cards, it seemed like it was the only plausible explanation.

I told Ellen I couldn't see exactly what was going to happen, but I emphasized that she must be very careful in all of her dealings for the next several months and to avoid anything that might put her in harm's way. Without a second thought, Ellen laughed off my warnings and quickly moved on to another topic.

Sadly, three months later I was watching the evening news when it was announced that Ellen Abrams had been hit by a car while jogging on a road with high snowbanks and had died. I said prayers for her, remembering the ominous card spread.

It is now 22 years later, and I have done hundreds more Tarot readings. Thankfully, not one since has produced that same distressing message.

*"The miracle shortens time by collapsing it,
thus eliminating certain intervals within it."*

T1.II.6:9

I truly believe Ellen's life would have been spared had she heeded my strong cautions to be careful. If she decided to listen to the advice of the reading, she could have chosen to use an indoor track to do her jogging, thus miraculously avoiding the dangers of a snowy road.

" … the miracle … introduces an interval
from which the giver and receiver both
emerge farther along in time than they would
otherwise have been."

T1.II.6:3,4

The *Course* tells us that although all of time has already taken place, it is malleable and can be changed. Whole threads of past and future events can be undone and completely vanish. It is possible through the belief in miracles.

10

Existential Agony

"It is denial of the Spark that brings depression ..."

T10.5.2:5

"Depression is an inevitable consequence of separation."

WpI.41.1:2

"You cannot distort Reality and know what it is. And if you do distort Reality you will experience anxiety, depression, and ultimately panic, because you are trying to make yourself unreal."

T9.I.14:3,4

Throughout the decade following my revelatory experience, I continued to immerse myself in every metaphysical, spiritual, and psychological teaching available. I still didn't have the answers to my seemingly unanswerable questions, and I desperately needed them.

It appeared to me the love of God had little, if anything, to do with life on earth. Love seemed especially random and accidental. From the cruel and warlike nature of many humans, to the little hurts and everyday slights we inflict on each other, love was in short supply wherever I looked.

The more I thought about these conflicting issues, the more confused I became. I persisted in asking myself if the perfection of Heaven is all we need, why would God create a universe of matter where destruction, decay, and death continuously pursue us? And, why would He put us here when the glory of our true home holds nothing but peace, joy, and eternal life?

I nearly drove myself mad trying to understand the reasons behind the confounding paradox of why we live in a matter world where everything dies, and not in the eternity of heaven. I had moments of intense anguish when I was trying to understand why God would create such different dwellings for us, and why we were stuck in the hellish one.

After all of my sublime experiences, why was it I still did not understand life? Due to this unending confusion, I started to feel that my sanity was being compromised. Was I going insane? Or, maybe, I was already insane.

* * *

By June of 1993, I had been running the store and its side businesses for four years with little help. I had been hosting a myriad of weekly classes taught by myself and others (notably, two well respected local metaphysicians, Don Hayes and Art Samson), and I was booking psychic readings and hypnotherapy sessions for a steady stream of clients.

I also had completed the last few classes required for my degree and obtained a bachelor's in art with a business minor. And, in order not to let my newly minted diploma collect dust, I promptly began promoting my flair for graphics and was soon designing logos, flyers, and business cards for customers.

Not surprisingly, my tightly booked schedule began to take its toll, and by September I was exhausted. One day while staring out of the storefront window, I realized

with a shudder that I was deeply unhappy. The inces-
sant demands of a wildly overcommitted life combined
with the pressure of trying to corral an out-of-control
husband was overwhelmingly stressful.

Again, I had made a mistake in my choice of partner.
I thought that I had married a stable, down to earth
businessman, but instead got someone who was reliving
childhood.

His penchant for partying was unrivaled, and he practically lived in the local bars. We barely saw each other.

My unhappiness turned into depression when I
started to have problems with the sight in my right eye.
Since the age of fourteen, I had been blind in my left
eye after being hit in the face by a speeding baseball.
The eyesight could not be saved because there was too
much scarring on the delicate retinal tissues.

The ball not only damaged my retina, but it also se-
verely broke my nose. As a result, it developed a prominent
bump which I lived with until the age of nineteen, when I
was able to have the surgery that restored its original shape.

Now, years later, my good eye appeared to be dete-
riorating. I was seeing rainbows around every light, and
parts of my visual field were wavy, as if I was looking at life
from underwater. I went to numerous eye doctors, but
they all were stumped as to the nature of the problem.

This was unbearable, because as an artist who lived
to draw and paint, I needed at least one good eye to pursue the hobby about which I was so passionate.

To add to my growing misery, in July of that year I learned my mother was experiencing symptoms of significant dizziness and motor imbalance. I knew it was serious when she came home early from her trip to Ireland.

Six years before, my mom had been diagnosed with breast cancer and had undergone a mastectomy. After her operation, she told me that she had known for months prior to her diagnosis that something bad was going to happen to her. It didn't surprise me in the least she had foreknowledge of a coming crisis.

It had been obvious since I was young that my mother's psychic abilities were turned up high. I could never get away with anything, because she knew what I was going to do before I did it.

My mom also had frequent premonitory dreams. She would warn the family of upcoming problems, and her dream scenarios regularly came true. One day she told my brother, Brian, to be very careful when driving, because while dreaming the night before she had seen him in a car accident. The very next day, he came home and told us he had crashed his car due to another driver's mistake. We were relieved the accident was minor.

Whenever my father happened to come upon me and my mother sitting around a spread of Tarot cards, he would laugh and call us "the two seers." He was amused that we had an aptitude for divination, although his logical engineer's mind kept him from fully respecting our skills.

It was why he never took seriously the exceptional dreams and otherworldly visions I had disclosed to him over the years. (But, to his credit, he never discouraged my unusual leanings, either).

Despite my family's routine shrugging off of my own psychic occurrences, I never doubted my mother's ability to discern the future. When I asked how she knew something adverse was going to happen to her months before getting the cancer diagnosis, she relayed a chilling story:

One morning after my dad had left for work, my mom went back to sleep for a short while. When she woke up and glanced out her bedroom window, every single tree and bush in our backyard was filled with black birds. Not just a few birds perched here and there, but every branch in every tree was filled to capacity with the dark creatures. Unnerved, she ran to the front of the house, and all of the trees in our front yard were likewise overflowing with the eerily silent black forms. My mother said right there and then she knew that she was a goner.

When she came back from Europe and told me the vertigo prevented her from driving and performing other simple activities, it was because of that story I immediately had a foreboding feeling. Like everyone else who hears that sort of negative news, I tried to look brave and told her I was sure the doctors would cure it.

I tried to believe it myself until later that night when I awoke from an eerie dream. A man who looked exactly like Albert Einstein came to me and said my mother would live for only another six months. Brushing away classic drops of cold sweat from my forehead, I steadfastly prayed for it to be a dream of anxiety and not one of premonition.

In my younger years, my mother and I had many tense moments, largely owing to my defiance of her. But, it was also because I was overly sensitive, and she was so frequently like a steamroller barreling over my feelings. Empathy was not a big part of her personality, and I could never understand why she couldn't be more understanding.

Fortunately, my mom mellowed considerably as the years went by, and we grew much closer. In her best moments, she was loyal and supportive, charming and entertaining. She made the holidays sparkle and always made a big deal out of our birthdays.

All in all, she had been a good mother, and I didn't want to lose her so soon. She was a young 71 and could have many satisfactory years to come.

My mother was diagnosed with a brain tumor a month later. The cancer had returned and had metastasized from a spot on her breast bone to her brain.

The doctors were not optimistic. I knew this would be the end for her, and I was despondent. I was going to lose a highly influential person in my life, someone from whom I had learned many hard lessons, but loved fiercely, and it was agonizing to face.

Luckily, I managed to get coverage for the store and was able to spend almost every day of the last three months of my mom's life with her. I traveled twenty miles each way and was barely able to see the road, but I drove slowly and carefully, determined not to miss any of our remaining time together.

My mother died in December of 1993, and it was a terrifying death. During the last week, she was unable to talk or move, and it was apparent she was in tremendous pain despite her morphine drip. On the last day, my sister and I knew her death was imminent when her breathing became unusually slow and took on an odd gurgling sound. The nurse told us it was called the "death rattle."

My sister and I stood on either side of my mother's bed, each cradling her head and shoulders. The look on her face was one of stark fear, and we encouraged her to let go and not be afraid, even though we ourselves were genuinely frightened. We had never been present at anyone's last breath before.

After my mother's passing, my depression worsened uncontrollably and now included acute, disabling panic attacks and flashbacks of her death.

Every morning I would wake up and my mom's dead face would be hovering right there in front of mine. In witnessing her death, I felt like whatever innocence I previously had about life was ripped away forever. I no longer had protection from the awful realities of the world, and I was scared.

My identity seemed to be crumbling, dissolving. I was losing my eyesight along with my sense of self, and I walked around like a ghost in a shadowy void. I was vacant inside. Nothing about the world made sense, least of all death. The old questions came screaming back and bit ferociously at my psyche.

The raw fear I felt from being so disconnected from my rational mind produced horrendous nightmares. I was afraid to go to sleep and couldn't eat. I felt no substance as a person, and my interactions with other people were emotionless, perfunctory. Every time I tried to imagine my future, the only thing I saw was a thick, gray fog bank.

Eventually, I became so desperate I toyed with the idea of suicide. But, since there were no guarantees about anything in life, I could not be sure it would end my torment. Unlike many of my family members, I did not believe that consciousness ended with death. I had never believed in biblical hell, but for all I knew, my suffering might come with me wherever I wound up.

I doubted that if I chose suicide I would land back in Goldenhawk or in Heaven, where I really wanted to be. I knew that ending my life was not the efficient way to get back to either. And the last thing I wanted to do was mess up my chances of a quick return to spiritual paradise.

The thought of my family also helped to stop me from going any further with the idea. They loved me and would be devastated if I took my life. It was simply not an option.

* * *

11

Mind Healing

"The First Coming of Christ is merely another name for the Creation, for Christ is the Son of God. The Second Coming of Christ means nothing more than the end of the ego's rule and the healing of the mind."

T4.IV.10:1,2

*"… healing is the gift of those who are
prepared to learn there is no world, and can
accept the lesson now."*

WpI.132.7:1

Life continued to be intolerable until the spring of 1994, when things began to slowly improve. I was working with my last bit of inner reserves when I got some good news regarding my eyes.

I had been referred to an outstanding eye surgeon, Dr. Neal Zimmerman, who had a practice in Waterbury. He promptly diagnosed an exceedingly rare "oil droplet" cataract, and recommended surgery with a lens implant. Several weeks later I had successful eye surgery, and my vision was restored.

More good news came soon after that. One of the bookstore's long time customers, Judy Kozlowski, came in one day and asked if I would consider selling the store to her. She had known of my troubles and for months had wanted to help in some way but was unsure what to do.

That is, until she got a sign from spirit. Judy had been looking out her window the week before and saw a large golden bird swoop into her yard. She had never before seen a bird of that kind on her property and was amazed at how striking it was. She looked in her bird book and discovered it was a hawk.

The next morning Judy strongly felt compelled to walk to the spot where the hawk had landed. To her delight, a lovely gold and white striped feather lay on the ground.

The moment Judy picked it up, the thought entered her mind that she should buy the store from me. It became a persistent idea she could not get out of her head. Judy was convinced it was her spirit guide -- or mine -- who was talking to her, and she felt that she had better listen.

The idea was exciting to Judy. She was a well-heeled single lady with few activities to occupy her time except shopping and going to the casino. Owning and running a metaphysical store seemed glamorous to her, and she felt it would be a meaningful way to make a difference to the community.

Months before, I had considered putting the store up for sale but quickly vetoed the idea. I had too little energy to contemplate doing anything even remotely that stressful, so when Judy approached me with her proposal, I was surprised but really quite pleased. I asked her to give me a day to think about it, though I didn't need it. I, too, suspected my guide had arranged it, and like Judy, felt I had better listen.

The next day I came up with what I believed to be a fair price. Soon after, Judy's accountant inspected the store and approved the deal. We signed the paperwork and five years after its opening, Golden Hawk Book & Gift had a new owner.

* * *

My heart still ached from the loss of my mother, but with the return of my eyesight and minus the burden of the store, my depression gradually started to lift.

Upon my doctor's advice, I agreed to take Zoloft, and it was another Godsend. The daily flashbacks of my mother's face rapidly dissipated, and within a week my power of concentration and ability to think clearly and had greatly recovered. The scary feelings of depersonalization, which had tortured me incessantly, also disappeared, and I again was able to relate to others in a natural way.

By the end of that spring, life had regained a sense of normalcy, though the old, unanswered questions tugged at the edges of my mind with increasing urgency. I was still at a loss for answers but was also afraid that if I started thinking about our nonsensical world too deeply, my sanity would destabilize again.

I needed a distraction. I decided to enroll in a master's program for counselor education at a local university. I reasoned that full-time school and taking hypnosis clients in my spare time would occupy me sufficiently. I was used to being busy, and since I was feeling better, felt I could handle the ambitious schedule. The first class did not start until the fall, so I had a few months to relax and mentally prepare to embark on this new chapter in my life.

For the balance of the summer, I saw hypnotherapy clients, offered card readings, taught classes at the store, and carefully continued my pursuit of truth. Per my usual style, I searched out every spiritual treatise being published but was able to only partially accept each premise.

Maryann Williamson's *A Return to Love* was different. After reading the first couple chapters, a deep feeling of affirmation told me that I was finally on the right path. It was based on a book I had always kept in stock at the store: *A Course In Miracles*. *Return* explained *ACIM* in a way that made it accessible. It was the first explanation of *Course* philosophy that I understood, and I was hooked.

I bought a copy of *A Course In Miracles* from Judy, and the day I took it home discovered that Jesus Christ was the author. He had channeled it to a psychologist who worked at Columbia University in New York in the 1960s.

That afternoon I realized *ACIM* held the answers I had been seeking since childhood. I was perusing the book when an astonishing sentence caught my eye:

"There is no world!"

WpI.132.6:2

I was electrified. I had never considered this extremely radical concept before.

I was familiar with a similar idea, the "Maya" or "world of illusion," which is a doctrine of the Hindu religion. A ninth-century Indian sage described Maya as a delusional plane of thought and action upon which humankind functions which veils our genuine cosmic nature.

In the past, I had accepted this hypothesis but felt it was yet another theory which did not adequately explain the nature of the physical universe.

In contrast, "*There is no world!*" was a conclusive statement that changed everything, and I embraced it into the essence of my being. It was the answer I always had been looking for, and I was joyous.

The sentence following that revolutionary thought stated that the nonexistence of the world is the main concept the *Course* is attempting to have us learn, but not all of us are at a sufficient point to welcome it. I said to myself, "Well, I am!"

I knew that I would be healed because I had accepted the lesson, and I literally could feel the last dregs of depression and anxiety that lingered at the edges of my consciousness resolve immediately. I danced around the room and felt euphoric to know the Truth at last.

I spent the next few weeks reading *A Course In Miracles* and all related materials I could find. The prolific writings of Kenneth Wapnick, PhD, especially were helpful to my understanding of the *Course*. Ken had been there in the early days of its inception, and he had assisted scribe Helen Shuchman and her colleague, Hugh Thetford, with its editing and dissemination. Ken was the preeminent authority of *ACIM,* and he made its principles clear and easy to grasp.

I learned that the matter universe is nothing more than a dream we are all dreaming together. We fell asleep for a brief moment, forgot we were still in Heaven, dreamed up this crazy world, and became fearful of our loving God and Creator. Our collective ego dreamed of our perishable bodies and world in order to hide from a god we thought would destroy us.

Now I understood why I "saw" my body fold up and disappear during the Revelation. *We* are the ones who made up the physical body, pain and discomfort, disease, decay, destruction, and death, *not God!* No wonder the world had never made sense to me; *God did not create it.* The universe of matter is not real, nor is anything in it!

ACIM asks us not to deny our bodies or our experiences in this world, though. It teaches they can be used as learning aids to speed our understanding of the unreality of matter and reinforce our remembering that Heaven is our true home which we have never left.

And, as long as we believe we live here on earth, we should take care of our bodies and the bodies of others. As Ken Wapnick and Gary Renard has reminded us in their books and lectures, it is important we don't neglect the normal running of our everyday lives or the other ordinary things of earth while we learn they do not really exist.

*   *   *

12

Forgiveness Brings a Gift

"Make way for love, which you did not create,
but which you can extend. On earth this
means forgive your brother that the darkness
may be lifted from your mind."

T29.III.4:1,2

"Forgiveness recognizes what you thought your brother did to you has not occurred. It does not pardon sins and make them real. It sees there was no sin."

WpII.1.1:1-3

Not long after that time of monumental discovery, the healing of my thoughts put into focus several grievances I had locked away at the edges of my consciousness decades before. I realized that I had some forgiveness work to do before I could fully embrace the healing of my mind.

I spent the next couple years working on forgiving my parents, myself, my failed romances, and the earlier, hurtful periods of my life with the gentle guidance of *A Course In Miracles.*

My most intensive forgiveness work was focused on my mother's overly severe discipline, her favoritism of my siblings, my lack of appropriate clothing, her indifference to my suffering, my father's indifference to the whole situation, and my own foolish behavior.

Even though I didn't have nearly the amount of resentment toward my spouse and prior fiancé as I had toward my parents, I still felt that I needed to forgive them for not being the men I wanted them to be.

"… the first step in the undoing is to recognize
that you actively decided wrongly …"

T5.VII.6:3

The *Course* advised that the initial stage in the forgiveness process was to recognize I had made a mistake by choosing to carry a grudge and that the true source of my lack of peace was my belief the problem lay outside of myself and caused by someone else.

The second step was to bring my thoughts back to the moment at which I had come to this faulty conclusion.

The third step was to give my incorrect choice to foster a grievance to Jesus or the Holy Spirit who would then cancel it and remove all of its repercussions.

The *Course* called this method of forgiveness the undoing of errors and mistakes, rather than sins, and it is simple in theory, but I found it somewhat difficult to execute. It was distressing and painful to look directly at the negativity after all the years I had spent repressing it. Forgiveness was definitely not easy but became less of a struggle with consistent, daily practice.

In my quieter moments, I remembered to keep bringing the unhappy memories I had stored for so long in the hidden closet of my mind to Jesus and the Holy Spirit. They helped me burn away the bad feelings in the light of their Love, Truth, and Knowledge.

"To forgive is to overlook. Look then,
beyond error and do not let your perception
rest upon it ..."

T9.IV.1:2,3

Eventually I was able to overlook and forgive all the mistakes, let them go, and move on in a healthy way. The miracle of forgiveness was no more apparent in my life than during that time.

Releasing the resentments I had harbored was like a fresh breeze blowing through the hallways of my mind cleansing everything it touched.

*   *   *

Almost precisely at the conclusion of my extended exercise in forgiveness, I was given another wonderful blessing. My guide returned!

One morning I was in the kitchen making breakfast when I happened to glance out the window at my dog. Lady was acting strangely. She was leaping higher than I had ever seen her and was yipping loudly with excitement. The expression on her furry little face was one of sheer joy and elation.

I looked at what was animating Lady so much and was floored to see a huge shadow on the ground in the shape of a person, except its bottom half had the outline of a long robe rather than pant legs. I strained my neck around the window to see who was making that enormous shadow. I could not see who or what it was.

I ran to the back door and threw it open. Lady was still jumping high into the air and seemed to be playing with it.

Following its silhouette, I looked way down to the edge of the yard, but the shadow extended farther. I was unable to see the end of it, nor could I see anyone connected to it. I sprinted across my yard and through several others trying to find the shadow's source, but the search was fruitless.

When I returned, Lady was serenely waiting to be let into the house. I could not come up with a logical explanation as to what just happened. My only conclusion was that I had witnessed an event of miraculous origin.

Later that night I was speaking on the phone to a cousin who was interested in metaphysics. I told her I believed my guide had visited me that afternoon. My cousin responded,

"Did you see a shadow you couldn't explain?"

I gasped in total surprise and asked her how she could have possibly known about the shadow. She then said,

"I don't know why I said that. It came out of my mouth on its own. I didn't know you were going to tell me you saw a shadow."

We both marveled at this acknowledgement of spirit, and it was confirmation that my magnificent guide had indeed visited. I was overjoyed by the gift of his appearance and took it as a sign that I was on the right path.

*   *   *

Shortly after the astounding rendezvous with my guide, I looked at what was, and wasn't, working in my life.

I was able to calmly end my ten year marriage and move into my own place. I concentrated on excelling in my classes, and in three years had a master's degree in hand. I secured full-time employment in my field of study soon thereafter.

Once I had satisfied the intellectual side of my mind, I turned to nurturing my artist's soul. I began painting abstract landscapes and developed a unique style, which I call Post-Pointillism.

I was urged to show my paintings but was more interested in the process and pleasure of making them, than in their exhibition. It was simply another gift that blessed my life and made my soul sing.

Since then, I have spent many productive and happy years quietly practicing the principles of *ACIM* and enjoying my work, art, and the people around me. I've tried to make a difference in my tiny corner of our collective dream and hope to continue being of service to others for a long time.

I have been fortunate to achieve many smaller victories in life, but recently have felt a strong inner pressure to accomplish one last important personal goal: to write the memoir of my remarkable spiritual journey and to describe how my mind was healed by the timeless lessons of *A Course In Miracles.*

*   *   *

"Let us raise our hearts from dust to life, as we remember this is promised us, and that this Course was sent to open up the path of light to us, and teach us, step by step, how to return to the eternal Self we thought we lost."

WpI.rV.in.5:4

Part Two
The Wisdom of
A Course In Miracles

13

Understanding A Course In Miracles
in Fifteen Simple Points

"This is a course in miracles. It is a required course. Only the time you take it is voluntary. Free will does not mean that you can establish the curriculum. It means only that you can elect what you want to take at a given time. The course does not aim at teaching the meaning of love, for that is beyond what can be taught. It does aim, however, at removing the blocks to the awareness of love's presence, which is your natural inheritance. The opposite of love is fear but what is all-encompassing can have no opposite."

T.INTRO.1-8

I

God is Real, He Created Your Mind, and Jesus is Here to Teach Us this Truth

"God is the Giver of Life …"

T1.I.4:1

" … all the lamps of God were lit by the same Spark."

T10.IV.7:5

"God is not partial. All His children have His total Love…"

T1.V.3:2,3

God is our Creator and Father who loves us completely, and He created each of our minds with a Spark of Light from His Holy Thoughts.

"Jesus ... Is he the Christ? O yes, along with you. ... He will remain with you to lead you from the hell you made, to God. ... Walking with him is just as natural as walking with a brother whom you knew since you were born, for indeed, such he is."

C5.3:1.5:1,2,4,6

" ... Jesus is for you the bearer of Christ's single message of the Love of God."

C5.6:4

"This course has come from him because his words have reached you in a language you can love and understand."

M23.7:1

Jesus Christ is the author of *A Course In Miracles.* He brought it to us in English, a comfortable and well-known language.

Jesus tells us he did this to help us understand and believe that God is Real, and we are forever connected to God by our Spark.

II

Your Name is Christ, You are Part of God, and Heaven is Your Home

" ... for Christ is the Son of God."

T4.IV.10:1

Jesus teaches that all of our minds, whom God created, together comprise the Christ. We are also known as the Son, or Sonship.

"Heaven ... was created as the dwelling place of God's Son. You are not at home anywhere else, or in any other condition."

T10.V.11:3,4

"Heaven is your home and being in God it must also be in you."

T12.VI.7:7

Heaven is in both God and Christ, is the condition of the unity of God and Christ, and is our only true Home.

> *"God shares his Fatherhood with you who are his Son, for He makes no distinctions in what is Himself and what is still Himself. What He creates is not apart from Him, and nowhere does the Father end, the Son begin as something separate from Him."*

W132.12:3,4

> *"God is not in you in a literal sense; you are part of Him."*

T5.II.5:5

> *"Your identification is with the Father and with the Son. It cannot be with one and not the other. If you are part of one you must be part of the other, because they are One."*

T8.IV.8:6-8

The Christ is part of God's Mind. God and Christ exist with each other in the eternity of Heaven, and function in Heaven together as One.

III

Long Ago, Part of the Christ Wondered if there was Anything Other than God and Heaven

"Into eternity, where all is one, there crept a tiny, mad idea, at which the Son of God remembered not, to laugh."

T27.VIII.6:2

"The tiny tick of time in which the first mistake was made, ..."

T26.V.3:5

Within the infinity of Heaven, there seemed to occur a moment when part of our unified, One Mind as the Christ, wondered if there was something else besides our Home in God's Mind.

We then forgot to laugh at this absurd notion and took it seriously. Jesus calls this silly idea a mistake.

IV

This Thought Caused the Christ to Fall Asleep and Dream of Being Separate from God

"The special ones are all asleep, …"

T24.III.7:1

"You have chosen a sleep in which you have had bad dreams, but the sleep is not real..."

T6.IV.6:3

"...the separation, or the "detour into fear."

T2.I.2:1

"You have forgotten Him…"

T7.IV.4:4

As soon as the Christ took this mistaken thought seriously, we seemed to fall asleep, and dreamed that we had separated from God.

By falling asleep and forgetting our true home in God, we became fearful of Him.

"Before the separation, the mind was invulnerable to fear, because fear did not exist. Both the separation and the fear are miscreations..."

T2.III.2:2,3

"Guilt is a sure sign that your thinking is unnatural. Unnatural thinking will always be attended with guilt, because it is the belief in sin."

T5.V.4:8,9

Because of our belief that we had sinned against God by dreaming of being separate from Him, we not only felt very fearful, but also very guilty.

V

The Sleeping Christ then Dreamed
of Egos, Bodies, and the World

*"You dream of a separated ego and believe in a
world that rests upon it."*

T4.I.4:4

*"In this world, because the mind is split, the
sons of God appear to be separate. Nor do
their minds seem to be joined. In this illusory
state, the concept of an "individual mind"
seems to be meaningful."*

C1.2:1-3

Out of the fear and guilt we felt by believing we had
separated from God, we dreamed up an individual personality known as the ego. The ego is also referred to as
the split mind or wrong mind.

*"Each body seems to house a separate mind,
a disconnected thought, living alone and in
no way joined to the Thought by which it was
created."*

T18.VIII.5:2

To go with the ego, we also dreamed up the physical world and our bodies in order to hide from God, because we were now so fearful of Him.

VI

The Sleeping Christ Thinks Wrongly with the Ego and Perceives Only Illusions

"Wrong-mindedness listens to the ego and makes illusions; perceiving sin and justifying anger, and seeing guilt, disease, and death as real."

C1.6:1

"You are at home in God, dreaming of exile ..."

T10.I.2:1

Now, as seemingly separated individuals with split off ego-minds and bodies that die, we think we inhabit this matter world and conduct our lives here. This is known as wrong-mindedness.

Our fearful and wrong thinking allows us to believe in things God did not create, like death. But we are simply dreaming of living in a separated world, and in truth, still abide in Heaven.

VII

God has a Voice to Talk to the Sleeping Christ and It is Called the Holy Spirit

"The Holy Spirit is in you in a very literal sense."

T5.II.3:7

"The Holy Spirit is your Guide in choosing.
He is in the part of your mind that always
speaks for the right choice, because He speaks
for God."

T5.II.8:1,2

Jesus tells us that the Holy Spirit represents God and is inside our minds and guides us to make the choice for God.

"… the Holy Spirit … is part of the Holy
Trinity, because His Mind is partly yours and
also partly God's."

T5.III.1:2,4

God, Christ, and the Holy Spirit compose the Holy Trinity, and the Holy Trinity is the Divine Order of God.

VIII

God Uses the Holy Spirit to Correct Our Illusions

*"When you chose to leave Him, He gave you
a Voice to speak for Him, because He could no
longer share His knowledge with you without
hindrance. Direct communication was broken
because you had made another voice."*

T5.II.5:6,7

*"The Holy Spirit … is your remaining
communication with God, …"*

T.5.II.8:1,3

The Holy Spirit, who is God's Voice and speaks for Him, has traveled with us into our dream of separation as the Memory of God, and is continually reminding us of Heaven and of God's Love and Knowledge.

"The Holy Spirit is God's Answer to the separation; ..."

T.5.II.2:5

God created the Holy Spirit the very second that we, as a part of the Christ, fell asleep and believed we had separated from God and Heaven. God did this so He could still speak to us while we were dreaming of our separated state.

The Holy Spirit has the ability to both see us in Heaven as the Sparks of Light that we truly are, as well as perceive us as the physical bodies that we believe we are, inside the dream of our matter world.

IX

We are Thinking Rightly when
We Listen to the Holy Spirit

*"The mind can be right or wrong, depending
on the voice to which it listens. Right-
Mindedness listens to the Holy Spirit, …"*

C1.5:1,2

Listening to the Holy Spirit is known as Right-
Mindedness. At any time here in the illusory world, we
can choose to listen either to the Holy Spirit, or to the
wrong-mindedness of the ego.

X

We Remember God when We Listen to the Holy Spirit

"In the Holy Instant, in which you see yourself as bright with freedom, you will remember God."

T15.1.10:7

"Enlightenment is but a recognition, not a change at all."

WpI.188.1:4

The realization that our egos and the dreams our egos have made are not real and the separation from God has never occurred is called the Holy Instant or Enlightenment.

XI

The Holy Spirit Brought us the Plan of Atonement

"The full awareness of the Atonement, then, is the recognition that the separation never occurred."

T6.II.10:7

This awareness is the first step in what Jesus calls the Plan of Atonement, which the Holy Spirit also brought to us the second we fell asleep and dreamed we separated from God.

XII

Jesus is in Charge of the Plan of Atonement

"I am in charge of the process of Atonement,
which I undertook to begin."

T1.III.1:1

"I have said before that I am in charge of the
Atonement. This is only because I completed
my part in it as a man and can now complete
it through others."

T4.VI.6:5,6

Jesus informs us that he oversees the Plan of Atonement. This is because he was the first separated, individual ego-mind to have perfectly awakened to the ultimate Truth that we are dreaming and have never left Heaven, the real Home that God created for us.

XIII

Miracles of Forgiveness Unfold the Plan of Atonement

"Miracles are natural signs of forgiveness."

T1.I.21:1

"Forgiveness is the healing of the perception of separation."

T3.V.9:1

"Miracles are selective only in the sense that they are directed towards those who can use them for themselves. Since this makes it inevitable that they will extend them to others, a strong chain of Atonement is welded."

T1.III.9:1,2

Jesus instructs us that miracles are the means to fulfilling the Plan of Atonement.

*"Miracles are examples of right thinking,
aligning your perception with Truth as God
created it."*

T1.I.36:1

*" ... those who hold grievances will suffer
guilt, as it is certain that those who forgive
will find peace."*

WPI.68.3:2

When we give up our grievances against others through
the miracle of forgiveness, we acknowledge their "sins"
against us were merely part of our dream world, and in
reality have never happened at all.

*"What is sin, except a false idea
about God's Son?
Forgiveness merely sees its falsity, and therefore
lets it go."*

WPI.1.1:5,6

By being willing to let go of our false beliefs in sin, guilt,
and fear, we start to forgive ourselves and each other for
what we really haven't done -- separate from God.

XIV

The Plan of Atonement Undoes the Separation, and It Will Not Fail

"Here is the Atonement made complete, the world passed safely by and Heaven now restored."

WPL.161.1:4

When the last separated mind has accepted the Atonement and has become enlightened through forgiveness of the separation, it will signal that the Plan of Atonement has been completed.

The reason it will not fail is because it has been accomplished already. As mentioned in a prior chapter, all of time has gone by, and our individual part in the Plan is over.

But, since our minds are reviewing the illusory events of time as if they are still happening, we must consciously choose to shorten our review of these events through the forgiveness process.

XV

The Last Step will be Taken by God
When He Brings Us Back to Heaven

*"This is God's Final Judgment: "You are still
My holy Son, forever innocent, forever loving
and forever loved, as limitless as your Creator,
and completely changeless and forever pure.
Therefore awaken and return to Me."*

W-pI.10.5:1,2

As soon as the Plan of Atonement is complete, God will take the final step, reawakening our minds to the fullness of His Knowledge, and returning us to Him.

*   *   *

14

The Little Spark and the Great Rays of God's Thought System

"… His thought system is light. … The more
you approach the center of His thought system,
the clearer the light becomes."

T11.IN.3:2,4

*"If you but see the little Spark, you will learn
of the greater Light, for the Rays are there
unseen."*

T10.IV.8:3

Did you know that you are literally connected to God
and to all minds He created by a permanent and indestructible Spark and Rays of spiritual light?

Light is the thought system of God, and He created
your mind with a little Spark from His Loving and Holy
Thoughts. Because your Great Rays are anchored to the
Spark with which God created your mind, they are literally the extension of His Light from your Spark. Since
the light of the Great Rays is of a spiritual nature, they
cannot be seen with the body's eyes.

*"...true perception means that you never
misperceive and always see truly. More
simply, it means that you never see what does
not exist, and always see what does."*

T3.II.2:5,6

On very rare occasions you can see your own Great Rays.
These majestic Rays look like giant beams of transparent white light flowing from your forehead. When this

happens, you will be in the initial phase of a Revelation, and you will be seeing the Rays with a type of spiritual vision that *ACIM* refers to as true perception.

While in the midst of this sublime otherworldly event, you will not be aware of your physical body, nor will you miss it.

As your Revelation progresses to the next phase, true perception no longer will be necessary and will give way to direct knowledge and communion with God.

"When Revelation of your oneness comes, it will be known and fully understood, ... "

W.pI.169.10:2

When our revelatory union with God occurs, we will have complete Knowledge of Him and our place in Heaven. Any questions we have can only happen before or after, but not during the actual Revelation.

"As the ego would limit your perception of your brothers to the body, so would the Holy Spirit release your vision and let you see the Great Rays shining from them, ... It is this shift to vision that is accomplished in the Holy Instant. "

T15.IX.1:1,2

The *Course* also speaks of being able to see the Great Rays shine out from other people. When that happens, you will be seeing with true perception and witnessing a miracle.

Artist renderings of Jesus and other holy figures usually depict them with glowing auras and halos which represent their Great Rays shining forth from their Spark.

*   *   *

15

You are Made of Light

*"… the Son of God, who was created of
light and in light. The Great Light always
surrounds you and shines out from you."*

T11.III.4:6,7

*"Turn toward the light, for the Little Spark
in you is part of a Light so Great that it can
sweep you out of all darkness forever."*

T11.III.5:6

"The light came with you from your native home, and stayed with you because it is your own. It is the only thing you bring with you from Him Who is your Source."

WPI.188.1:6,7

You are composed solely of light and nothing else. Even though you believe that you are not presently in your heavenly homeland, you have brought the light of your Spark and Great Rays with you into your dream of darkness. This is because your light is never apart from you and *cannot be* apart from you.

"The Holy Spirit is in light because He is in you who are light, but you yourself do not know this."

T5.III.7:6

"Child of Light, you know not that the light is in you."

T13.VI.10:1

"Ask for light and learn that you are light. If you want understanding and Enlightenment you will learn it, because your decision to learn it is the decision to listen to the Teacher Who knows of light, ..."

T8.III.1:3,4

You have forgotten you are made of light because of your belief that you have separated from God. Your wish to become enlightened is what brings the knowledge that you are made only of light.

This understanding is not bestowed on you without first deciding you want it, and you learn it by your right-minded decision to listen to the Holy Spirit, the Teacher within you.

*   *   *

16

Holy Spirit, Mediator

"The Holy Spirit mediates higher to lower
communication, keeping the direct channel
from God to you open for Revelation.
Revelation is not reciprocal. It proceeds from
God to you, but not from you to God."

T1.II.5:3-5

"And so He keeps this channel open to receive
His communication to you, …"

T15.VIII.5.5

The Holy Spirit communicates with you through a direct link from God's Mind to yours, and He keeps this communication channel open in order that you may experience Revelation.

He maintains the pathway by keeping your memory of God alive. It remains open, no matter how much you allow your fearful ego to surround it with clouds of faulty and detrimental thinking.

Revelation always begins with God, and it flows to you from Him. This is because He created you, and not the other way around. You get ever closer to attaining it whenever you choose to listen to the gentle Voice of the Holy Spirit and not to the harsh voice of the ego.

After a sustained time period of listening to the Holy Spirit more than to your ego, you will eventually be able to achieve spiritual vision, see your own Great Rays, and experience Revelation and Enlightenment.

*   *   *

17

Jesus, Facilitator

"Revelations are indirectly inspired by me because I am close to the Holy Spirit, and alert to the Revelation-readiness of my brothers. I can thus bring down to them more than they can draw down to themselves."

T1.II.5:1,2

"I have said already that I can reach up and bring the Holy Spirit down to you, but I can bring him to you only at your own invitation."

T5.I.3:2

In essence, Jesus is saying that he is the secondary force who inspires Revelations (the first force being the Holy Spirit).

He does this by drawing down to your mind the love, knowledge, and light of God and the Holy Spirit as soon as you show him you are ready for it and have invited it.

Jesus brings this holy light down through the indestructible connection God's Mind has to yours. He is able to do this because the eternal channel linking you to God is kept open by the Holy Spirit.

Jesus is always alert to your ability to experience Revelation. Because of his vigilance, he knows the moment when you are ready, and he facilitates it. He can do this because he is always mindful of how many right-minded, loving thoughts you are thinking at any one time.

Thus, Jesus is immediately aware of the second that your miraculous thoughts outnumber your fearful thoughts on all levels of your consciousness.

When this happens, the clouds surrounding the pathway which connects you to your Creator become less dense, and it allows Jesus to readily conduct God's Light down to you via the Holy Spirit.

*   *   *

18

The Ego and the Obscurity of the Great Rays

"In many only the Spark remains for the Great Rays are obscured. Yet God has kept the Spark alive so that the Rays can never be completely forgotten."

T10.IV.8:1,2

*"The closer you come to the foundation of the
ego's thought system, the darker and more
obscure becomes the way. Yet even the little
Spark in your mind is enough to lighten it."*

T11.In.3:5,6

"Remember the Rays that are there unseen."

T11.In.3:3

The hurtful ideas of separation, sin, anger, hatred, evil, murder, death, guilt, and fear are nurtured in your wrong mind, the home of the ego.

Repeatedly choosing to think on the wrong side of your mind is what keeps you believing in the darkness of the ego's disturbed thought system, and is what distracts you from the love, joy, and light of God.

Due to this wrong-minded thinking, the knowledge of your magnificent Spark and Great Rays is hidden from your awareness. Because of its belief in insane ideas, your destructive, fear-ridden ego has effectively veiled the Great Rays from your sight.

*"If you give no power to the fog to obscure the
light, it has none."*

T12.II.2:2

In contrast, there are no foggy clouds of negative ideas in your right mind, the home of the Holy Spirit. Whenever you choose to think with your right mind, you are listening to Him.

If you do this enough, you will eventually become aware that your divine channel to and from God is clear, and in reality, had been obscured only by the fog of your bad dreams.

It is the choice for right thinking that paves the way for Jesus to facilitate a Revelation for you. In order to experience this direct union with God, you must consistently choose to dispel your ego's dark clouds of negativity which seem to block your path to Him and conceal your Great Rays.

*   *   *

19

The Miracle of Bringing
Your Light to Others

*"God does not need Revelation returned to
Him, which would clearly be impossible, but
He does want it brought to others. ... through
the attitudes the knowledge that the Revelation
brings."*

T4.VII.7:3,5

*"Revelation unites you directly with God.
Miracles unite you directly with your brother."*

T1.II.1:5,6

"Your mind is so powerful a light that you can look into theirs and enlighten them, as I can enlighten yours."

T7.V.10:6

The knowledge you attain through Revelation can be reflected to other people by your enlightened frame of mind.

"The mind we share is shared by all our brothers, and as we see them truly they will be healed. Let your mind shine with mine upon their minds, ... to make them aware of the light in them."

T7.V.11:2,3

Jesus is referring to the fact that, together as the Sonship of Christ, we share our minds which are all connected by the spiritual light of our individual Sparks.

Jesus asks you to perform the miracle of enlightening others in our dream world by combining your mind's light with his and acknowledging the light in theirs.

" ... everything that comes from love is a miracle."

T1.I.3:3

Your choice to do this is a miracle because it is a loving act. In turn, it helps others to accept the truth of their light, which moves them farther along their own path to Revelation and Enlightenment.

"When you offer a miracle to any of my
brothers, you do it to yourself and me."

T1.III.1:2

Because each of our minds is like a single element of a vast hologram, what happens in one of our minds reverberates throughout the whole.

Whenever you choose to listen to Jesus and the Holy Spirit and gift another person with the miracle of forgiveness or Enlightenment, you are actually gifting everyone, including yourself and Jesus.

"Ask me which miracles you should perform."

T1.III.4:3

" ... the action aspect of the miracle should
be controlled by me because of my complete
awareness of the whole plan. ... only I am in the
position to know where they can be bestowed."

T1.III.8:4,5

You are also instructed to first ask Jesus before attempting a miracle, because only he knows where it is best applied.

> *"... the non-rightminded, or the sick, ... are already in a fear-weakened state. If they are prematurely exposed to a miracle, they may be precipitated into panic."*

T2.IV.4:7-9

Not everyone on whom you want to work a miracle may be able to accept your light and love. Some people are frightened of love, forgiveness, or Enlightenment because of the flawed and misguided beliefs of their fearful egos.

> *"Miracles are a way of earning release from fear. Revelation induces a state in which fear has already been abolished. Miracles are thus a means and Revelation is an end."*

T1.I.28:1-3

Despite there being a number of people who are still afraid of miracles, choosing to help Jesus perform miracles through you is actually the way to reduce, and eventually eliminate, the fear in your own mind.

The more you devote and dedicate yourself to giving and receiving miracles, the less power fear will have over your mind and the closer you will come to gaining or "winning" a Revelation.

> *"...under my guidance miracles lead to the*
> *highly personal experience of Revelation."*

T1.III.4:5

Repeatedly being a willing conduit for miracles, under the direction of Jesus, will inevitably lead to your personal revelatory experience.

> *"When you return to your original form of*
> *communication with God by direct Revelation,*
> *the need for miracles is over."*

T1.I.46:3

Miracles will no longer be necessary when the dreaming part of your mind fully awakens and you are once again communicating with God directly.

20

Preparing for Revelation

*"The Revelation that the Father and the Son
are One will come in time to every mind. "*

WPI.158.2:8

" ... the Revelation of the Father and Son
as One has been already set. ... the mind
determines when that time will be, and has
determined it."

WpI.169.4:1,2

"Its coming is ensured."

WpI.169.14:4

We are promised by Jesus that someday each of us will experience Revelation, and the part of our minds which is outside the ego-made illusions of time and space already knows when we will gain this profound experience and become enlightened.

It is difficult to be certain when it will occur, as our egos are afraid of Oneness with God and deliberately try to block our progress with negative thinking and the other complicated distractions of our daily lives. However, when we choose with right-minded persistence to listen to the Divine Voice within, we can shorten the wait considerably.

"The injunction "Be of one mind" is the
statement for Revelation-readiness."

T2.V.A.17:1

Universal consciousness, or being of "one mind," is a prerequisite for earning Revelation.

When we open our minds to the higher learning of *A Course In Miracles,* or similar thought systems, work with diligence to let go of our prejudices and grievances by forgiving others, and cherish a sincere wish to live in peace and cooperation with all beings in the universe, we will be well on our way to securing the mindset needed for this transcendental experience.

> " ... *accept the gifts that grace provided*
> *you. You carry them back to yourself. And*
> *Revelation stands not far behind."*

WpI.169.14:1-3

Whenever we make the conscious choice to live our lives according to these elevated principles, Revelation and Enlightenment will not be too far away.

> *"Only the healed mind can experience*
> *Revelation with lasting effect, because*
> *Revelation is an experience of pure joy."*

T5.I.1:3

We become enlightened during Revelation by the recognition that we have neither left Heaven nor separated from God.

Afterward, the acceptance of this joyous Knowledge means our mind has been healed and we have taken our rightful place in the Holy Spirit's Plan of Atonement.

"Seek not within the world to find your Self.
Love is not found in darkness and death. Yet
it is perfectly apparent to the eyes that see and
ears that hear Love's Voice."

WpI.127.6:1-3

All of Heaven's Love, Knowledge, Light, and Truth is quietly awaiting your discovery, anytime you choose to look for it and listen to it.

*   *   *

In Memoriam

During the writing of this book, a very special person and Advanced Teacher of God who inestimably influenced my life for the better chose to leave this dream world we call Earth:

Kenneth Wapnick, PhD
Author, Lecturer, Beloved Teacher at the
Foundation for A Course In Miracles, Temecula, CA

Thank you, Ken, for everything you taught to your grateful student. Your gifts have been innumerable to me, and to the thousands of *ACIM* students across the world who have been enlightened and enriched by your tireless work, kind words of encouragement, and playful humor poking fun at our seriousness and belief in dreams. Your brilliant light will always burn bright in our hearts and minds.

Additional Dedication
I'd also like to dedicate this book to my wonderfully supportive family and friends as well as in loving memory of my parents.

Additional In Memoriam
Another important person who changed my life passed while I was writing this book: My eye doctor, Dr. Neal Zimmerman. Thank you, Dr. Zimmerman, for giving me back the gift of sight. You will always be remembered for your gentleness and amazing expertise.

Website
Please visit my website, DawnofGoldenhawk.com to leave questions or comments or to order prints of my original, Post-Pointillism Artwork.

Reference Key

T – Text of *A Course In Miracles*
    in – introduction
W – Workbook
    pI and pII – part I and part II
M – Manual for Teachers
C – Clarification of Terms

For Example:
T1.II.2:1,2 = Text Chapter 1. Section II. Paragraph 2: Sentences 1 and 2

Printed in Great Britain
by Amazon

52460034R00111